Classroom
MANAGEMENT
that works

Research-Based Strategies for Every Teacher

Robert J. Marzano

with Jana S. Marzano & Debra J. Pickering

Association for Supervision and Curriculum Development
Alexandria, Virginia USA

Association for Supervision and Curriculum Development
1703 N. Beauregard St. • Alexandria, VA 22311-1714 USA
Telephone: 800-933-2723 or 703-578-9600 • Fax: 703-575-5400
Web site: http://www.ascd.org • E-mail: member@ascd.org

Gene R. Carter, *Executive Director*; Nancy Modrak, *Director of Publishing*; Julie Houtz, *Director of Book Editing & Production*; Tim Sniffin, *Project Manager*; Reece Quiñones, *Senior Graphic Designer*; Cynthia Stock, *Typesetter*; Vivian Coss, *Production Specialist*

All Web links in this book are correct as of the publication date below but may have become inactive or otherwise modified since that time. If you notice a deactivated or changed link, please e-mail books@ascd.org with the words "Link Update" in the subject line. In your message, please specify the Web link, the book title, and the page number on which the link appears.

Printed in the United States of America.

September 2003 member book (pcr). ASCD Premium, Comprehensive, and Regular members periodically receive ASCD books as part of their membership benefits. No. FY04-1.

ISBN: 0-87120-793-1   ASCD product no.: 103027
ASCD member price: $20.95   nonmember price: $25.95

Library of Congress Cataloging-in-Publication Data

Marzano, Robert J.
   Classroom management that works : research-based strategies for every
teacher / Robert J. Marzano with Jana S. Marzano and Debra J. Pickering.
      p.   cm.
Includes bibliographical references and index.
   ISBN 0-87120-793-1 (alk. paper)
   1. Classroom management—United States. 2. Effective teaching—United
States. I. Marzano, Jana S. II. Pickering, Debra. III. Title.

LB3013.M365   2003
   371.102'4—dc21   2003013237

13 12 11 10 09 08 07 06 05 04   12 11 10 9 8 7 6 5 4 3 2

Contents

1

THE CRITICAL ROLE OF CLASSROOM MANAGEMENT

Teachers play various roles in a typical classroom, but surely one of the most important is that of classroom manager. Effective teaching and learning cannot take place in a poorly managed classroom. If students are disorderly and disrespectful, and no apparent rules and procedures guide behavior, chaos becomes the norm. In these situations, both teachers and students suffer. Teachers struggle to teach, and students most likely learn much less than they should. In contrast, well-managed classrooms provide an environment in which teaching and learning can flourish. But a well-managed classroom doesn't just appear out of nowhere. It takes a good deal of effort to create—and the person who is most responsible for creating it is the teacher.

We live in an era when research tells us that the teacher is probably the single most important factor affecting student achievement—at least the single most important factor that we can do much about. To illustrate, as a

result of their study involving some 60,000 students, S. Paul Wright, Sandra Horn, and William Sanders (1997) note the following:

> The results of this study will document that the most important factor affecting student learning is the teacher. In addition, the results show wide variation in effectiveness among teachers. The immediate and clear implication of this finding is that seemingly more can be done to improve education by improving the effectiveness of teachers than by any other single factor. *Effective teachers appear to be effective with students of all achievement levels regardless of the levels of heterogeneity in their classes.* If the teacher is ineffective, students under that teacher's tutelage will achieve inadequate progress academically, regardless of how similar or different they are regarding their academic achievement. (p. 63) [emphasis in original]

Researcher Kati Haycock (1998) uses the findings of this study and others conducted by William Sanders and his colleagues (e.g., Sanders & Horn, 1994) to paint a dramatic picture of the profound impact an individual teacher can have on student achievement. The point is illustrated in Figure 1.1, which depicts the differences in achievement between students who spend a year in class with a highly effective teacher as opposed to a highly ineffective teacher.

According to Figure 1.1, students in the classes of teachers classified as the most effective can be expected to gain about 52 percentile points in their achievement over a year's time. Students in the classes of teachers classified as least effective can be expected to gain only about 14 percentile points over a year's time. This comparison is even more dramatic when one realizes that some researchers have estimated that students will

exhibit a gain in learning of about 6 percentile points simply from maturation—from growing one year older and gleaning new knowledge and information through everyday life (see Hattie, 1992; Cahen & Davis, 1987). The least effective teachers, then, add little to the development of students' knowledge and skill beyond what would be expected from simply growing one year older in our complex, information-rich society.

Sanders and his colleagues, who gathered their data from elementary school students in Tennessee, are not the only ones to document dramatic differences in achievement between students in classes taught by highly ineffective versus highly effective teachers. Haycock (1998) reports similar findings from studies conducted in Dallas and Boston.

I have come to similar conclusions in my work, although I have taken a very different approach from that used in the studies that form the basis for Haycock's conclusions. Whereas the studies conducted in Tennessee, Dallas, and Boston were based on data acquired from students over time, I used a research process called meta-analysis to synthesize the research on effective schools over the last 35 years (see Marzano, 2000a, 2003b). That approach enabled me to separate the effect on student achievement of a school (in general) from the effect of an individual teacher. Figure 1.2 illustrates my findings.

To understand the impact that a teacher can make, let's consider each of the five scenarios in Figure 1.2. (For a detailed discussion of how the computations in Figure 1.2 were derived, see Marzano, 2000a.) As depicted in Figure 1.2, if a student begins at the 50th percentile in mathematics, let's say, and attends an average school and has an average teacher, her achievement will still be at the 50th

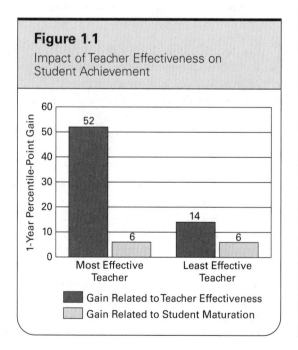

Figure 1.1

Impact of Teacher Effectiveness on Student Achievement

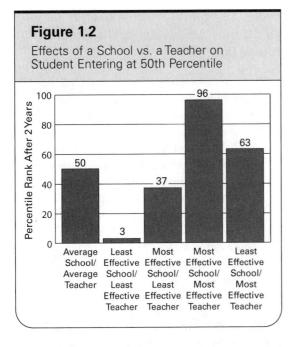

Figure 1.2

Effects of a School vs. a Teacher on Student Entering at 50th Percentile

in the class of a teacher classified as most effective. She enters the class at the 50th percentile, but she leaves at the 96th percentile. The fifth scenario most dramatically depicts the impact of an individual teacher. Again, the student is in a school that is considered least effective, but she is with a teacher classified as most effective. The student now leaves the class at the 63rd percentile—13 percentile points higher than the point at which she entered. It is this last scenario that truly depicts the importance of individual teachers. Even if the school they work in is highly ineffective, individual teachers can produce powerful gains in student learning.

Although the effect the classroom teacher can have on student achievement is clear, the dynamics of how a teacher produces such an effect are not simple. Rather, the effective teacher performs many functions. These functions can be organized into three major roles: (1) making wise choices about the most effective instructional strategies to employ, (2) designing classroom curriculum to facilitate student learning, and (3) making effective use of classroom management techniques.

The first role deals with instructional strategies and their use. Effective teachers have a wide array of instructional strategies at their disposal. They are skilled in the use of cooperative learning and graphic organizers; they know how best to use homework and how to use questions and advance organizers, and so on. Additionally, they know when these strategies should be used with specific students and specific content. Although cooperative learning might be highly effective in one lesson, a different approach might be better in another lesson. Some general strategies that have a good research "track record" in terms of enhancing student achievement have

percentile at the end of about two years. The student has learned enough to keep pace with her peers. But what happens to that student if she attends a school that is considered one of the least effective and is unfortunate enough to have a teacher who is classified as one of the least effective? After two years she has dropped from the 50th percentile to the 3rd percentile. She may have learned something about mathematics, but that learning is so sporadic and unorganized that she has lost considerable ground in a short time. In the third scenario, the same student is in a school classified as most effective, but she has a teacher classified as least effective. Although the student entered the class at the 50th percentile, two years later she leaves the class at the 37th percentile. In contrast to the two previous scenarios, the fourth presents a very optimistic picture. The student is not only in a school classified as most effective, but also is been detailed in *Classroom Instruction That Works: Research-Based Strategies for Increasing Student Achievement* (Marzano, Pickering, & Pollock, 2001).

The second role associated with effective teaching is classroom curriculum design. This means that effective teachers are skilled at identifying and articulating the proper sequence and pacing of their content. Rather than relying totally on the scope and sequence provided by the district or the textbook, they consider the needs of their students collectively and individually and then determine the content that requires emphasis and the most appropriate sequencing and presentation of that content. They are also highly skilled at constructing and arranging learning activities that present new knowledge in different formats (e.g., stories, explanations, demonstrations) and different media (e.g., oral presentations, written presentations, video presentations, Web-based presentations, simulations, hands-on activities).

The third role involved in effective teaching is classroom management. This, of course, is the subject of this book. The following chapters detail and exemplify the various components of effective classroom management.

Before delving into classroom management, however, it is important to note that each of these three roles is a necessary but not sufficient component of effective teaching. That is, no single role by itself is sufficient to guarantee student learning, but take one out of the mix and you probably guarantee that students will have difficulty learning. Nevertheless, a strong case can be made that effective instructional strategies and good classroom curriculum design are built on the foundation of effective classroom management. As Long and Frye (1985) note in their

book, *Making It Till Friday: A Guide to Successful Classroom Management,* it is a myth to believe that

> . . . effective teachers can prevent all discipline problems by keeping students interested in learning through the use of exciting classroom materials and activities. The potential for problems exists beyond academics. Students experience difficulties at home which spill over into the classroom; students experience problems with peers during class breaks and in the classroom which often involve the teacher; and students experience mood changes which can generate problems, to name just a few. (pp. 3–4)

Similarly, in their synthesis of the research, Edmund Emmer, Julie Sanford, Barbara Clements, and Jeanne Martin (1982) note that

> At all public school grade levels, effective classroom management has been recognized as a crucial element in effective teaching. If a teacher cannot obtain students' cooperation and involve them in instructional activities, it is unlikely that effective teaching will take place . . . In addition, poor management wastes class time, reduces students' time on task and detracts from the quality of the learning environment. (p. 13)

A Brief History of Classroom Management Research

It is probably no exaggeration to say that classroom management has been a primary concern of teachers ever since there have been teachers in classrooms. However, the systematic study of effective classroom management is a relatively recent phenomenon. Here we briefly consider the major studies on classroom management. (For more detailed and comprehensive discussions, see Emmer, 1984; Brophy, 1996; and Doyle, 1986, 1990.)

Arguably, the first high-profile, large-scale, systematic study of classroom management was done by Jacob Kounin (1970). He analyzed videotapes of 49 first and second grade classrooms and coded the behavior of students and teachers. Kounin's findings are discussed in more depth in Chapter 5, but it is worth noting here that he identified several critical dimensions of effective classroom management. Those dimensions (among others) are (1) "withitness," (2) smoothness and momentum during lesson presentations, (3) letting students know what behavior is expected of them at any given point in time, and (4) variety and challenge in the seatwork assigned to students. "Withitness" involves a keen awareness of disruptive behavior or potentially disruptive behavior and immediate attention to that behavior; of the four dimensions, it is the one that most consistently separates the excellent classroom managers from the average or below-average classroom managers.

In 1976 Brophy and Evertson reported the results of one of the major studies in classroom management, up to that point, in a book entitled *Learning from Teaching: A Developmental Perspective*. Their sample included some 30 elementary teachers whose students had exhibited consistently better than expected gains in academic achievement. The comparison group consisted of 38 teachers whose performance was more typical. Brophy and Evertson's study, then, might be considered a comparison of exceptional teachers with average teachers. Although the study focused on a wide variety of teaching behaviors, classroom management surfaced as one of the critical

aspects of effective teaching. Much of what they found relative to classroom management supported the earlier findings of Kounin. Brophy and Everson (1976) say this about their study:

> Much has been said . . . in the book about our findings concerning classroom management. Probably the most important point to bear in mind is that almost all surveys of teacher effectiveness report that classroom management skills are of primary importance in determining teaching success, whether it is measured by student learning or by ratings. Thus, management skills are crucial and fundamental. A teacher who is grossly inadequate in classroom management skills is probably not going to accomplish much. (p. 27)

A series of four studies conducted at the Research and Development Center for Teacher Education in Austin, Texas, marked a milestone in the research on classroom management. The first study involved 27 elementary school teachers. The second involved 51 junior high school teachers. Results from the elementary school study were reported in Emmer, Evertson, and Anderson (1980) and Anderson, Evertson, and Emmer (1980). Results from the junior high study were reported in Evertson and Emmer (1982) and in Sanford and Evertson (1981). Both studies were descriptive and correlational in nature and identified those teacher actions associated with student on-task behavior and disruptive behavior. Again, Kounin's earlier findings were strongly supported. One of the more significant conclusions from these studies was that early attention to classroom management at the beginning of the school year is a critical ingredient of a well-run classroom.

The third and fourth studies, also conducted in the elementary and junior high schools, respectively, examined the impact of training in classroom management techniques based on findings from the first two studies. The findings from these studies were reported by Emmer, Sanford, Clements, and Martin (1982); Emmer, Sanford, Evertson, Clements, and Martin (1981); and Evertson, Emmer, Sanford, and Clements (1983). As described by Emmer (1984),

> In the later two studies, the interventions occurred at the beginning of the school year and resulted in improved teacher behavior in many, but not all, management areas and also in more appropriate student behavior in experimental group classes as compared to control group classes . . . (p. 17)

Together, these studies set the stage for research and practice in classroom management for the late 1980s through the 1990s and resulted in two books on classroom management: one for the elementary level (Evertson, Emmer, & Worsham, 2003) and one for the secondary level (Emmer, Evertson, & Worhsham, 2003); both are now in their sixth edition. To date, these books have been considered the primary resources for the application of the research on classroom management to K–12 education.

The Classroom Strategy Study conducted by Jere Brophy (see Brophy, 1996; Brophy & McCaslin, 1992) was the next major study addressing classroom management. It involved in-depth interviews with and observations of 98 teachers, some of whom were identified as effective managers and some of whom were not. The study presented teachers with vignettes regarding specific types of students (e.g., hostile-aggressive students, passive-aggressive students, hyperactive students) in specific situations. Among the many findings from the study was that effective classroom managers tended to employ different types of strategies with different types of students, whereas ineffective managers tended to use the same strategies regardless of the type of student or the situation. One of the study's strong recommendations was that teachers should develop a set of "helping skills" to employ with different types of students. (Chapter 4 presents the implications of Brophy's study in more depth.)

In spite of the profound impact of these various studies, classroom management received its strongest endorsement in a comprehensive study by Margaret Wang, Geneva Haertel, and Herbert Walberg (1993). They combined the results of three previous studies. One involved a content analysis of 86 chapters from annual research reviews, 44 handbook chapters, 20 government and commissioned reports, and 11 journal articles. This analysis produced a list of 228 variables identified as having an impact on student achievement. The second study involved a survey of 134 education experts who were asked to rate each of the 228 variables in terms of the relative strength of their impact on student achievement. The third study involved an analysis of 91 major research syntheses. The end result of this massive review was that classroom management was rated *first* in terms of its impact on student achievement.

In summary, the research over the past 30 years indicates that classroom management is one of the critical ingredients of effective teaching. Many studies and many books have been published articulating the specifics of effective classroom management. So what does this book have to offer that has not already been established? Certainly, this book reinforces the findings and suggestions from many of the previous works. However, the recommendations in this book are based on a new research methodology not previously employed with the classroom management literature per se. That methodology is meta-analysis.

Meta-Analysis and Classroom Management

Meta-analysis is an approach to research that was formally developed by researcher Gene Glass and his colleagues (see Glass, 1976; Glass, McGaw, & Smith, 1981) in the early 1970s. In simple terms, it is a technique for quantitatively combining the results from a number of studies. Since its inception, it has been used extensively in the fields of education, psychology, and medicine. The powerful impact that meta-analysis has made on these fields of study is chronicled in the book *How Science Takes Stock: The Story of Meta-Analysis* by Morton Hunt (1997).

In effect, this research technique has allowed us to construct generalizations about education, psychology, and medicine that were previously not available. A logical question is, Why is the simple act of combining the findings from a number of studies so powerful? The answer is that any single study, no matter how well constructed, will have "uncontrolled error" influencing its outcomes. To illustrate, let's consider a well-designed study that examines the impact of a specific classroom management strategy on students' behavior. The study might randomly assign students to two groups—one that uses the strategy (the experimental group) and one

that does not (the control group). The study might ensure that both groups do everything exactly the same except for the classroom management strategy that is being studied. Even with this level of tight control, the findings that come from the study might be influenced by uncontrolled error. For example, the way student behavior is measured might not be sensitive to behaviors that are important to the study; something might happen to the students in the experimental or the control group that is not related to the study but influences their behavior, and so on.

In fact, it is almost impossible to control all the error that might creep into a study. This is why researchers assign a probability statement to their findings. When researchers report that their findings are significant at the .05 level, they are saying that there is a very small chance—less than 5 chances in 100—that their findings are a function of the uncontrolled error in the study. When researchers report that their findings are significant at the .01 level, they are saying that there is as an even smaller chance that the findings are a function of uncontrolled error—less than 1 chance in 100. By combining the results of many studies, we can say with far more certainty than we can with a single study that certain strategies work or do not work. This concept is considered again in more detail in Chapter 2.

To write this book, I undertook a meta-analysis that included the findings from more than 100 separate reports. I discuss, in nontechnical terms, the results of that meta-analysis throughout the book, and they form the foundation for my recommendations. (See the Appendix for a more detailed discussion of the meta-analysis and Marzano, 2003a, for a technical description.)

As shown in Figure 1.3, my meta-analysis addressed four general components of effective classroom management: (1) rules and procedures, (2) disciplinary interventions, (3) teacher-student relationships, and (4) mental set. The remaining chapters of this book address these factors (along with some others) in depth. However, let's briefly consider the meaning of the scores presented in Figure 1.3. The fourth column indicates the number of studies that were examined for each of the four components. The third column reports the total number of students involved in those studies. The second column presents the average effect size for each of the four general components of classroom management.

An *effect size* is a metric used in meta-analyses. In the context of this book, it tells you how much of a difference in behavior you can expect between classes that effectively employ a given aspect of classroom management and classes that do not. To illustrate, let's consider the average effect size for disciplinary interventions, as shown in Figure 1.3.

It is −.909. This average was computed using the findings from 68 studies involving 3,322 students. An average effect size of −.909 can be interpreted to mean that in classes where disciplinary procedures were used effectively, the average number of classroom disruptions was .909 standard deviations *less than* the average number of disruptions in classrooms that did not effectively employ disciplinary procedures.

One of the benefits of using the effect size metric is that we can translate it into a percentile change relative to the average number of disruptions that occur in a classroom. Let's think of a disruption as any type of student behavior not sanctioned by the teacher. A disruption can be as innocuous as a student talking to her neighbor or as severe as a student being disrespectful to the teacher. So, for this example, we are not distinguishing the severity of disruptions, only the number of disruptions. What does an effect size of −.909 for disciplinary interventions tell us? In this case, an effect size of −.909 translates into a

---

Figure 1.3

Meta-analysis Results for Four Management Factors

Factor	Average Effect Size	Number of Subjects	Number of Studies	Percentile Decrease in Disruptions
Rules and Procedures	−.763	626	10	28
Disciplinary Interventions	−.909	3,322	68	32
Teacher-Student Relationships	−.869	1,110	4	31
Mental Set	−1.294	502	5	40

Note: All effect sizes are significant at the .05 level.

decrease of 32 percentile points relative to the average number of disruptions in class. (For a discussion of how effect sizes are translated into percentile changes, see the Appendix.) This means that the average number of disruptions in classes where disciplinary interventions are employed effectively will be at the 18th percentile in terms of the distribution of disruptions in classes where disciplinary interventions are not employed effectively.

To further understand the distribution of disruptive behavior, consider Figure 1.4. Let's assume that the average number of disruptions per day is 10 in classes where disciplinary interventions are not employed and that the standard deviation is 5.0. This is depicted in the distribution on the right of Figure 1.4. Given what we know about normal distribu-

tions, this implies that some days there will be many more disruptions than 10. In fact, we can predict that on some days the number of disruptions will be two standard deviations (or more) above the mean. That is, on some days there will be 20 disruptions in these classrooms. Conversely, some days the number of disruptions will be two standard deviations below the mean—some days there will be no disruptions. In other words, the classes that don't employ disciplinary interventions will have a few "low-disruption days" and a few "high-disruption days," but the average number of disruptions will be 10 per day. Now let's consider the distribution on the left of Figure 1.4, which represents the classes that use disciplinary interventions effectively. Here the mean is 5.46 and the standard deviation is

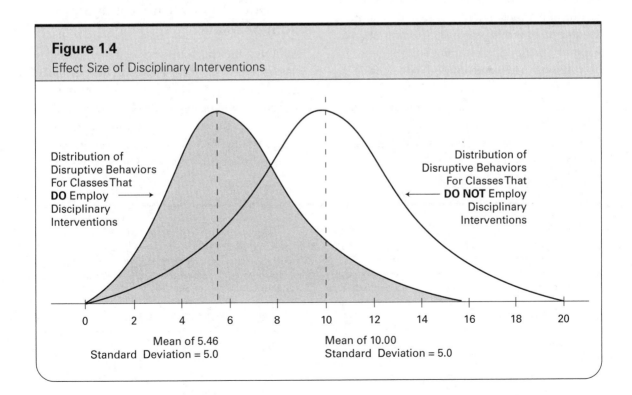

Figure 1.4
Effect Size of Disciplinary Interventions

Distribution of Disruptive Behaviors For Classes That **DO** Employ Disciplinary Interventions ⟶

⟵ Distribution of Disruptive Behaviors For Classes That **DO NOT** Employ Disciplinary Interventions

0   2   4   6   8   10   12   14   16   18   20

Mean of 5.46
Standard Deviation = 5.0

Mean of 10.00
Standard Deviation = 5.0

again 5.0. On high-disruption days, these classes will have 15.46 disruptions. On low-disruption days these classes will have none.

In summary, Figure 1.4 indicates that classes that use disciplinary interventions will have their good days and bad days, as will classes that don't. However, the average number of disruptions in classes that use disciplinary interventions effectively is substantially fewer than in classes that don't. Over a year's time, this decrease in disruptive behavior results in a significantly different atmosphere in the two types of classes. Over a year's time, classes that employ disciplinary interventions will have about 980 disruptions, whereas classes that do not will have about 1,800.

The effect sizes reported in Figure 1.3 make a strong case that effective use of classroom management techniques can dramatically decrease the disruptions in your classes. The results of my meta-analysis also demonstrate the impact of effective use of classroom management strategies on student engagement and student achievement (see Figure 1.5).

Figure 1.5 reports that classes in which effective classroom management techniques are used have engagement rates for students that are .617 standard deviations higher than the engagement rates in classes where effective management techniques are not employed. This translates into a 23-percentile-point increase in engagement. Figure 1.5 also indicates that classes with effective classroom management techniques reach achievement levels that are .521 standard deviations higher than the achievement in classes without effective classroom management techniques. This translates into a 20-percentile-point increase in achievement. In other words, my meta-analysis indicates that, on the average, students in classes where effective management techniques are employed have achievement scores that are 20 percentile points higher than students in classes where effective management techniques are not employed. By a number of measures, then, effective classroom management has a powerful impact on students.

Are Good Classroom Managers Born or Made?

Although the characteristics of an effective classroom manager are clear and even somewhat intuitively obvious, what might not be as clear or obvious is how you become an effective classroom manager. You might ask the question, Are effective classroom managers born, or can you become one if you are

Figure 1.5
Effects of Classroom Management on Engagement and Achievement

Outcome	Average Effect Size	Number of Subjects	Number of Studies	Percentile Increase
Engagement	+.617	784	7	23
Achievement	+.521	553	5	20

Note: All effect sizes are significant at the .05 level.

not one already? Fortunately, the answer to this question is that effective classroom managers are made. Good classroom managers are teachers who understand and use specific techniques. Awareness of and training in these techniques can change teacher behavior, which in turn changes student behavior and ultimately affects student achievement positively. Again, research evidence supports this assertion.

To illustrate, consider the research by Walter Borg and Frank Ascione (1982). In a study involving 34 elementary school teachers who were randomly assigned to experimental and control conditions, they found that (1) teachers who had been trained in the use of effective classroom management techniques (the experimental group) improved their use of those techniques when compared to a group of untrained teachers (those in the control group), and (2) the students of the teachers in the experimental group had fewer disruptions and higher engagement rates than those in the control groups.

One of the most promising findings from the research on becoming a skilled classroom manager is that apparently it can happen relatively quickly. For example, in their study of some 40 junior high school teachers randomly assigned to experimental and control groups, Emmer, Sanford, Clements, and Martin (1982) found that teachers' skills at classroom management could be significantly improved even by the simple intervention of providing them with a manual and two half-day workshops. As described by Emmer and his colleagues,

> The experimental treatment in the study was mainly informational, with no opportunity for feedback, directed practice, diagnosis with targeted intervention, or continued support and encouragement from staff or colleagues. Thus the treatment conforms to the type noted . . . as a minimal intervention . . . (p. 65)

Similar findings were reported for minimal interventions for elementary school teachers by Emmer, Sanford, Evertson, Clements, and Martin (1981).

How This Book Is Organized

The seven remaining chapters in this book cover various aspects of classroom management in greater detail. Chapter 2 addresses classroom rules and procedures. Chapter 3 discusses disciplinary interventions. Chapter 4 addresses teacher-student relationships, and Chapter 5 addresses mental set. Chapter 6 provides a different perspective on classroom management. Instead of considering what the teacher can do to enhance the management of the classroom, it considers the role of the student in the effective management of the classroom. In effect, it discusses student responsibility for classroom management. Chapter 7 considers how to begin the school year in a way that ensures a good start to management. Finally, in a shift from the individual-classroom perspective of Chapters 2 through 7, Chapter 8 considers the role of the school in the business of management.

Each chapter begins with a consideration of the research and theory. Next, specific programs that are particularly strong in a given aspect of classroom management are considered. The heart of each chapter is a section entitled "Action Steps." These are specific recommendations for you, the classroom teacher.

Summary

Clearly, individual classroom teachers can have a major impact on student achievement. Of the three roles of the classroom teacher—making choices about instructional strategies, designing classroom curriculum, and employing classroom management techniques—classroom management is arguably the foundation. Research on classroom management supports this argument, as does the meta-analysis on which this book is based.

2

RULES AND PROCEDURES

Probably the most obvious aspect of effective classroom management involves the design and implementation of classroom rules and procedures. Emmer, Evertson, and Worsham (2003) attest to the need for rules and procedures by explaining that they

> . . . vary in different classrooms, but all effectively managed classrooms have them. It is just not possible for a teacher to conduct instruction or for students to work productively if they have no guidelines for how to behave or when to move about the room, or if they frequently interrupt the teacher and one another. Furthermore, inefficient procedures and the absence of routines for common aspects of classroom life, such as taking and reporting attendance, participating in discussions, turning in materials, or checking work, can waste large amounts of time and cause students' attention and interest to wane. (p. 17)

Even though this quotation comes from a textbook on secondary classroom management, the authors make the same assertion about elementary rules and procedures (Evertson, Emmer, & Worsham, 2003).

Although the terms are sometimes used interchangeably, rules and procedures have some important differences. Both refer to stated expectations regarding behavior. However, a rule identifies general expectations or standards, and a procedure communicates expectations for specific behaviors (Evertson et al., 2003; Emmer et al., 2003). For example, a teacher might establish the rule "Respect others and their property." This single rule addresses a wide range of expected behaviors. The same teacher might also establish separate procedures for collecting assignments, turning in late work, participating in class discussions, and so on. These expectations are fairly specific in nature.

The Research and Theory

As discussed in Chapter 1, the findings from my meta-analysis form the basis for the recommendations made in this book (although I have tried to also include the findings and conclusions from a broad and, I hope, representative review of the research and theory). Figure 2.1 presents the results of the meta-analysis with regard to rules and procedures.

The first row in Figure 2.1 reports the average effect size for designing and implementing classroom rules and procedures in general. Out of 10 studies involving 636 students, the average effect size was –.763. Figure 2.1 also reports the average effect sizes for designing and implementing rules and procedures at the high school level, the middle school/junior high level, and the upper

elementary level. Before considering those grade-level effect sizes, let's focus on the average effect size of –.763.

This effect size indicates that across the various grade levels the average number of disruptions in classes where rules and procedures were effectively implemented was 28 percentile points lower than the average number of disruptions in classes where that was not the case. Figure 2.1 also includes information that was not presented in the discussion in Chapter 1 regarding effect sizes—namely the column entitled 95 Percent Confidence Interval. That interval for the average effect size of –.763 is –.598 to –.927. Understanding what this interval means will help broaden the discussion of the benefits of meta-analysis.

Recall that in Chapter 1 I described meta-analysis as a technique for quantitatively synthesizing the findings from a number of studies. In this case, the findings from 10 studies were synthesized to produce the average effect size of –.763 for rules and

Figure 2.1
Effect Sizes for Rules and Procedures

	Average Effect Size	95% Confidence Interval	Number of Subjects	Number of Studies	Percentile Decrease in Disruptions
Design and Implementation of Rules and Procedures	–.763	(–.598) to (–.927)	636	10	28
High School	–.772	(–.574) to (–.970)	425	3	28
Middle School/Junior High	–.617	(–.059) to (–1.293)	48	1	23
Upper Elementary	–.772	(–.438) to (–1.106)	163	6	28
Primary	ND	ND	ND	ND	ND

ND = No data were available to compute an effect size.

procedures. In Chapter 1, I noted that meta-analysis allows us to be more certain of our findings. This is because of the increased number of students who are involved in a meta-analysis as opposed to a single study. In terms of the design and implementation of rules and procedures, the average effect size reported in Figure 2.1 involved 636 students across 10 studies. Any one of those studies probably involved about 60 students. When researchers have only 60 students in a study, they typically won't have a great deal of confidence in their findings. The effect size they observe might be rather large, but this might be due to the uncontrolled error mentioned in Chapter 1. For example, students in the class where rules and procedures were implemented might have been less disruptive by their very nature than students in the class that did not implement rules and procedures. In general, the more subjects included and the more studies considered, the more this uncontrolled error tends to cancel itself out and findings become more reliable.

In Figure 2.1, the level of certainty for each average effect size is reported in the 95 percent confidence interval. That interval reports the range of effect sizes in which we are 95 percent sure that the "real" effect size would be found if a study contained no error. Consequently, Figure 2.1 tells us that we are 95 percent sure that the smallest the real effect size could be for implementation of rules and procedures (if there were no uncontrolled error in a study) is –.598, and the largest it could be (if there were no uncontrolled error in a study) is –.927. In other words, we are still not sure that the reported average effect size of –.763 is uncontaminated by error. It might be artificially high, or it might be artificially low. But we can say with 95 percent cer-

tainty that the real effect size is probably no smaller than –.598 and probably no larger than –.927. This provides us with a great deal of confidence that designing and implementing classroom rules and procedures has a definite effect on student behavior. In fact, any confidence interval that does not include 0.00 is referred to as "significant at the .05 level."

In Figure 2.1, none of the confidence intervals include 0.00; therefore, the effect sizes are significant at the .05 level. As you read the remaining chapters of this book, you will note (by examining the 95 percent confidence intervals) that all of the effect sizes reported from my meta-analysis are significant at the .05 level. In fact, only one of the effect sizes even comes close to zero, and that single effect size appears in Figure 2.1. To further illustrate the concept of a confidence interval, let's consider that one outlier effect size in more depth.

As reported in Figure 2.1, the average effect sizes for the high school, middle school/junior high, and upper elementary levels are –.772, –.617, and –.772, respectively. (No data were available to compute an average effect size for the primary level.) All of these are substantial. Based on the discussion above, we know that all three of these average effect sizes are significant at the .05 level because their confidence intervals do not include 0.00. However, even though the confidence interval for the middle school/junior high level does not include 0.00, it comes close; it ranges from –.059 to –1.293. This means that we are 95 percent sure that the real effect of rules and procedures on student behavior at the middle school/junior high level might be as large as –1.293 or as small as –.059. This is a very large range and doesn't provide as much confidence in our average effect size for the middle school and junior high levels as we have with the other levels. The reason why we have less confidence in this average is readily apparent in Figure 2.1. That average of –.617 was based on one study involving 48 students. It is because we have so few subjects in this study that we must establish a wide confidence interval around our average. Does this mean that we should question whether rules and procedures are effective at the middle school level? Certainly not. It is still significant at the .05 level, which is the typical standard in educational research. Additionally, given the pattern of effect sizes reported throughout this book, I can confidently say that if one more study could have been found on the impact of rules and procedures at the middle school level, the confidence interval would be much smaller simply because we had more students with which to compute an average.

This situation does, however, illustrate the underlying logic and power of meta-analysis. When you combine the results from a number of studies, you can say with increasing confidence that a given classroom management technique (or any other technique you might be studying) has a specific impact on student behavior or achievement.

In addition to the effect sizes reported in Figure 2.1, the importance of rules and procedures is evident from the research on the home environment. For example, in a study involving more than 69,000 pairs of parents and children, Xitao Fan and Michael Chen (2001) found an effect size of .26 for the impact of establishing rules and procedures at home on student academic achievement. This means that establishing rules and procedures at home is associated with a 10-percentile-point increase in student achievement at school. It might be the case that proper use of

rules and procedures at home fosters dispositions in students that help them behave better in school and consequently learn more. Similarly, in a study involving more than 2,000 high school students, Ellen Slicker (1998) computed an effect size of –.79 for the impact of implementing rules and procedures at home on student behavior in school. This means that effective use of rules and procedures at home is associated with a decrease in disruptive behavior at school of 29 percentile points. Similar findings have been reported by a number of other researchers (Christenson, Rounds, & Gorney, 1992; Martini, 1995).

Clearly, the research supports the notion that designing and implementing rules and procedures in class and even at home has a profound impact on student behavior and on student learning. However, research also indicates that rules and procedures should not simply be imposed on students. Rather, the proper design of rules and procedures involves explanation and group input. This was demonstrated in a study by Brophy and Evertson (1976) in which they compared the instructional techniques of teachers who consistently produced student achievement gains greater than expected to the techniques of a group of randomly selected teachers. They note,

> . . . the more successful teachers took pains to explain both the rule itself and the reason behind it to the children. This was important in helping the children to see the need for the rule and therefore, to accept it . . . In contrast to this middle of the road system with good explanations and built-in flexibility, the less well organized and successful teachers tended to have either no rules at all (so that they were continually making *ad hoc* decisions that

distracted them from teaching tasks), or else to have so many rules that the rules became overly specific and essentially meaningless. (pp. 58–59)

In their book, *Discipline with Dignity,* Richard Curwin and Allen Mendler (1988) also comment on the importance of student input when establishing classroom rules and procedures. They go so far as to say that classroom rules and procedures should be viewed as a "contract" (p. 47) between teacher and students.

Again, the research on home atmosphere also supports the need for a negotiated, rather than an imposed, set of rules and procedures. Slicker's (1998) study indicates that negotiated rules and procedures at home have an effect size of –.47 on student behavior in school when compared with rigidly imposed rules and procedures. This means that the implementation of negotiated rules and procedures between parents and children results in an 18-percentile-point decrease in student misbehavior at school as compared to rigidly imposed rules and procedures at home.

Research and theory, then, support the intuitive notion that well-articulated rules and procedures that are negotiated with students are a critical aspect of classroom management, affecting not only the behavior of students but also their academic achievement.

Programs

Virtually all of the programs on classroom management address to some degree the four factors associated with classroom management as described in this book. Specific programs typically emphasize some aspects more than others. In this section, I briefly summarize the characteristics of a program that is particularly strong in the implementation of rules and procedures. Other chapters have a similar section discussing programs that are particularly strong in their respective classroom management topics.

One of the most well-researched classroom management programs is the Classroom Organization and Management Program (COMP), developed by Carolyn Evertson and her colleagues at Vanderbilt University (see Evertson, 1995; Evertson & Harris, 1999). In addition to its strong emphasis on rules and procedures, the program addresses techniques for organizing the classroom, developing student accountability, planning and organizing instruction, conducting instruction and maintaining momentum, and getting off to a good start.

COMP has a particularly strong track record in terms of its impact on students. Specifically, a number of studies have shown that COMP decreases student disruptive behavior, increases student engagement, and even increases student achievement as measured by standardized tests at both the elementary and secondary levels. (See Evertson, 1995 for a review.)

According to Evertson (1995), COMP is designed to be an inquiry-based approach to staff development for K–12 educators. During the 6 to 18 weeks of inservice training, teachers analyze their classroom practice using a series of checklists, try out research-based strategies, and examine the effectiveness of their efforts. Textbooks used in the course include *Classroom Management for Elementary Teachers* (Evertson et al., 2003) and *Classroom Management for Secondary Teachers* (Emmer et al., 2003). According to Evertson (1995), "Since 1989, COMP has trained over 5,870 teachers and administrators in 28 states/territories and gained over 2,900 adoptions" (p. 7).

ActionSteps

ACTION STEP 1 ▼

Identify specific rules and procedures for your classroom.

As mentioned previously, different classrooms will have different rules and procedures depending on the needs and dispositions of the teacher and the students. However, teachers typically use rules and procedures in the following general categories:

- General expectations for behavior
- Beginning and ending the class day or the period
- Transitions and interruptions
- Materials and equipment
- Group work
- Seatwork and teacher-led activities

This does not mean that you must have rules and procedures in each of these areas. In fact, doing so would probably be counterproductive. Indeed, Emmer, Evertson, and Worsham (2003) recommend that teachers employ only about seven rules and procedures at the secondary level. Evertson, Emmer, and Worsham (2003) recommend only from five to eight at the elementary level. Thus, it is important that you carefully select the rules and procedures for your classroom.

▶ General Classroom Behavior

Most situations involve general expectations about how we treat others and how they treat us. The same is true for the classroom. Rules and procedures should be established for general conduct and behavior in a variety of contexts.

At the elementary level, rules and procedures for general classroom behavior commonly address the following areas:

- Politeness and helpfulness when dealing with others
- Respecting the property of others
- Interrupting the teacher or others
- Hitting or shoving others (see Doyle, 1986; Evertson et al., 2003; Good & Brophy, 2003).

To illustrate how rules and procedures for general classroom behavior might be approached at the elementary level, consider the following vignette:

During the first week of school, Mr. Banner divided his 3rd graders into groups and gave each group one of the four major rules for the class. The task for the students was to print the rule on a strip of paper and decorate the strip with simple pictures related to the rule. As they worked, they were to discuss the theme of the rules, which was thoughtful behavior. The rules read as follows:

1. Help two classmates a day; think of others.

2. Treat the property of others as if it belonged to you; think about how you would feel.

3. Listen to others before speaking; think before you speak.

4. Keep your hands to yourself; think before you act.

Periodically, Mr. Banner took a strip down from the wall and discussed with the students how "thinking" could help them understand and obey the rules.

When necessary, the class added an additional rule on a new strip of paper, always stating it in "thinking" terms.

At the secondary level, rules and procedures for general behavior commonly address the following areas:

- Bringing materials to class
- Being in the assigned seat at the beginning of class
- Respecting and being polite to others
- Talking or not talking at specific times
- Leaving the assigned seat
- Respecting other people's property (see Emmer et al., 2003; Brophy, 1996; Doyle, 1986; Good & Brophy, 2003)

The following vignette portrays how a secondary teacher might initially approach rules and procedures for general classroom behavior:

Ms. Sweeney, the 9th grade English teacher, had two goals during the opening week of school—to communicate with students about the class rules and to introduce the major curriculum units for the first quarter. She decided that it would be fun to address both of those goals at once—by using poetry, one of the first curriculum units, to communicate the rules. Her students received a handout with the following simple poem that she had composed:

> *Bring your paper, pencils, books,*
> *Unless you want my dirty looks.*
> *Class will start—I know I'm pushy—*
> *When in your seat, I see your "tushy."*
>
> *You need to know that it's expected*
> *That you respect and feel respected.*
> *Watch your words and be polite,*
> *Avoid aggression, please don't bite.*

> *Sometimes you'll sit, sometimes you'll walk,*
> *Sometimes you'll listen, sometimes you'll talk.*
> *Please do each of these on cue.*
> *Listen to me, I'll listen to you.*
>
> *These rules exist so we can learn.*
> *Obey them and rewards you'll earn.*
> *I also feel compelled to mention,*
> *Breaking rules will mean detention.*
>
> *If these rules seem strict and terse,*
> *Please make suggestions, but only in verse.*

Just as she had hoped, the students chuckled when they read the poem. This created a lighthearted feeling in the room as she went over each verse with them, expanding on the meaning of the rules. When she posted the poem on the bulletin board in the front of the room, she was convinced that the students' feelings about the rules were more positive than she had seen in the past, when she had simply posted a sterile list of rules. And there was a bonus—she felt ready to begin her unit on using poetry as a way of communicating ideas and feelings.

▶ Beginning of the School Day or Beginning of the Period

The manner in which class begins sets the tone for what happens next. Beginning well is particularly important in a self-contained classroom where students begin and end the day with the same teacher or in the same room. When the day is organized in classes taught by different teachers, the manner in which each class begins is critical. Consequently, rules and procedures might be set for the beginning of the day and the beginning of the period. The same might be said for the end of the day or the end of the period. The way the day or the period ends leaves students with an impression that carries over to the next time you meet.

At the elementary level, rules and procedures that pertain to the beginning and ending of the school day commonly address the following areas:

• Beginning the school day with specific social activities (e.g., acknowledging birthdays, important events in students' lives)
• Beginning the day with the Pledge of Allegiance
• Doing administrative activities (e.g., taking attendance, collecting lunch money)
• Ending the day by cleaning the room and individual desks
• Ending the day by putting away materials (see Evertson et al., 2003; Doyle, 1986; Brophy, 1996; Good & Brophy, 2003)

To understand how these rules and procedures might be employed, consider the following vignette:

Ms. Patton had established routines for her 2nd graders that helped them to begin and end the day efficiently, thus maximizing instructional time. When students entered the class, they immediately walked over to a pegboard where colorful name chips were hanging. Students removed their name chips and placed them in boxes that indicated their lunch preference. As soon as they sat down they immediately began to work on the "sponge" problem on the board, a problem that was always both challenging and fun. While they were working, Ms. Patton recorded absences by checking which name chips were still hanging on the board and prepared the lunch count by

counting the chips in the lunch-preference boxes. No time was wasted, and the stage was set for a productive day. At the end of the day, students placed their chips back on the board as soon as they had cleaned up and put away materials. When all the chips were back on the board, Ms. Patton dismissed the class.

At the secondary level, rules and procedures that pertain to the beginning and ending of class commonly address the following areas:

• Taking attendance at the beginning of the period
• At the beginning of the period, addressing students who missed the work from the previous day because of absence
• Dealing with students who are tardy at the beginning of the period
• Ending the period with clear expectations for homework (see Emmer et al., 2003; Doyle, 1986; Brophy, 1996; Good & Brophy, 2003)

The following vignette depicts how one teacher addressed this area:

Mr. Lima's routines for starting and ending class were designed to get the most from the 47-minute period and to shift some of the management responsibilities to the students. To achieve this, students were organized into groups with specific roles assigned on a rotating basis. One student in each group took on the role of "Organizer." During the first minute of class, the Organizer's job was to check with each group member to determine if anyone needed make-up assignments explained and to ensure that everyone had the required materials for class. Mr. Lima, at the same time, scanned the room to mark attendance and tardies in his grade book. Within a minute or two, the students and Mr. Lima were ready to begin working. At the end of class, the Organizer was given time to make sure that everyone had recorded and understood the homework. If problems or confusion occurred that could not be addressed within the group, the Organizer asked Mr. Lima for assistance. This group approach, in Mr. Lima's opinion, helped to ensure that students' individual needs were addressed immediately, which minimized the potential for classroom disruptions.

▶ Transitions and Interruptions

Inevitably students will have to leave and enter the classroom for a variety of reasons. For example, individual students might have to leave your classroom to use the bathroom, to go to the office, and so on. Additionally, the whole class might leave to attend a school-wide function, to go to the library, and so on. These transitions and interruptions can cause chaos without relevant rules and procedures.

At the elementary level, rules and procedures that pertain to transitions and interruptions commonly address the following areas:

- Leaving the room
- Returning to the room
- Use of the bathroom
- Use of the library and resource room
- Use of the cafeteria
- Use of the playground
- Fire and disaster drills
- Classroom helpers (see Evertson et al., 2003; Doyle, 1986; Brophy, 1996; Good & Brophy, 2003)

The following vignette depicts how transitions and interruptions might be addressed at the elementary level:

Inside the classroom door, Mr. Swanson had a large flip chart with laminated pages. Each page had a list of rules and procedures for the major transitions that would regularly occur, such as going to the bathroom, to recess, and to assemblies. In the margins of each list were pictures, created by his students each year, that illustrated the most important part of each rule and procedure. Before major transitions, Mr. Swanson would ask a student to flip to the appropriate page and then lead the class in a review of the rule or procedure. Periodically, after a class transition, Mr. Swanson would flip to the appropriate page and ask specific students to lead the class in an evaluation of the students' behavior. This gave him the opportunity to both reinforce good behavior and to address problems. When the front page of the flip chart was showing, students saw the simple general reminder, "What should I be doing right now?"

At the secondary level, rules and procedures that pertain to transitions and interruptions commonly address the following areas:

- Leaving the room
- Returning to the room
- Fire and disaster drills
- Split lunch period (see Emmer et al., 2003; Doyle, 1986; Brophy, 1996; Good & Brophy, 2003)

To understand how these areas might be introduced at the secondary level, consider the following vignette:

When she was talking about safety procedures and rules, Ms. Bono found that it was as difficult to get the attention of her high school students as it was for flight attendants to get the attention of frequent fliers when safety procedures were being explained. One year she ran across an old copy of a film that had been shown to her decades before, which showed students crouching under their desks in case of a nuclear attack. She decided to show this to her students to get their attention and make them laugh. It worked. The students were awake and attentive by the end of the film. She began, "We are going over some major class procedures here. You have seen some differences in what I had to do when I was in school. As you listen, be ready to tell me which procedures are probably the same as those I heard when I was in school—and which ones are probably dramatically different.

▶ **Use of Materials and Equipment**

Materials and equipment are critical to a variety of subject areas. Most subject areas use textbooks, and many require other materials such as lab equipment, artistic materials, computer-related equipment, and so on. Commonly, rules and procedures apply to retrieving and replacing these materials.

At the elementary level, rules and procedures that pertain to the use of materials and equipment commonly address the following areas:

- Distributing materials
- Collecting materials
- Storage of common materials
- The teacher's desk and storage areas
- Students' desks and storage areas
- The use of the drinking fountain, sink, and pencil sharpener (see Evertson et al., 2003; Doyle, 1986; Brophy, 1996; Good & Brophy, 2003)

To understand how these rules and procedures might be addressed at the elementary level, consider the following vignette:

One of the major roles assigned in Mr. Brayson's cooperative groups was "Materials Captain." Each week, the student in the group who was assigned this role took responsibility for handing out and collecting materials throughout the school day. To ensure that all students understood this role, Mr. Brayson taught the students the distinctions for each of the three major areas where materials might be kept. He labeled these areas Yours, Mine, and Ours. Yours referred to the materials in students' own desks, materials that the Captains were not to touch. Mine referred to materials that belonged to Mr. Brayson and that were not to be used by students. Ours referred to all other classroom materials that would be distributed and collected by the Materials Captain. All of the students, when it was their turn to be Captain, understood the importance of these distinctions, and that Mr. Brayson expected them to follow his procedures. "You are the Captains, but remember, I am the Admiral," Mr. Brayson often joked.

At the secondary level, rules and procedures that pertain to the use of materials and equipment commonly address the following:

- Distributing materials
- Collecting materials
- Storage of common materials (see Emmer et al., 2003; Doyle, 1986; Brophy, 1996; Good & Brophy, 2003)

To understand how these rules and procedures might be addressed at the secondary level, consider the following vignette:

Mr. Teller had learned from years of experience that even high school science students need close monitoring at the beginning and end of science labs to make sure equipment is distributed, and then collected and stored properly. To help him with this monitoring, he asked the photography instructor to take pictures of the storage areas when all equipment was put in its proper place. These pictures were printed up as posters and hung on the wall next to each storage area as a guide and a reminder for students to put equipment away properly. Periodically Mr. Teller covered up one or two of the pictures with a humorous or bizarre picture he found on the Internet. If the students in charge of storing equipment in each area did not notice the new picture and comment on it, he knew they had stopped using the photos to check proper equipment storage. He would then gently but firmly remind them to use the pictures every time they stored equipment.

▶ Group Work

Group work—particularly cooperative group work—is a powerful instructional activity. Indeed, research indicates that cooperative learning groups have a positive impact on student achievement, interpersonal relationships, and attitudes about learning (see Slavin, 1995; Johnson & Johnson, 1999; Nastasi & Clements, 1991). These positive benefits are usually attributed to students' increased interaction with the content and with each other. For cooperative learning to produce these positive results, it must be set up well via the implementation of relevant rules and procedures.

Rules and procedures pertaining to group work at the elementary level commonly address the following areas:

- Movement in and out of the group
- Expected behaviors of students in the group

- Expected behaviors of students not in the group
- Group communication with the teacher (see Evertson et al., 2003; Doyle, 1986; Brophy, 1996; Good & Brophy, 2003)

The following vignette depicts how one teacher approached group work:

Ms. Westerberg had avoided using group work in her classroom for years, until she took a workshop on how to maximize group time. As a result of the workshop, she realized that, in the past, she had never made group behavioral expectations clear to the students. Now, whenever she uses group work, she spends time at the beginning and end of each work session going over the rules and then processing with students how well the rules worked for the groups. For example, one rule, "Two before me," is intended to remind students to ask each other for help before coming to the teacher. On the first day of a new group project, Ms. Westerberg reminds students of this rule and explains the importance of helping each other. At the end of their work time each day, she asks the students to describe in their individual learning logs any example of how they (1) received help from their group members and (2) might have helped each other better. Every day, before they begin working, the students read to their group members the learning log entry from the previous work session. This starts their work with a review of what is going well and what behaviors need to be improved.

Rules and procedures pertaining to group work at the secondary level commonly address the following areas:

- Movement in and out of the group
- Group leadership and roles in the group

- The relationship of the group to the rest of the class or other groups in the class
- Group communication with the teacher (see Emmer et al., 2003; Doyle, 1986; Brophy, 1996; Good & Brophy, 2003)

To understand how these areas might be addressed at the secondary level, consider the following vignette:

Ms. Frost and Ms. Savory agreed that they were enjoying teaching their 8th graders so much this year because they were team teaching. One of the main advantages to teaming was that they could role-play behavioral expectations for the students, dramatizing both appropriate and inappropriate behavior. For example, when using cooperative learning groups, they would assign roles, such as recorder, timekeeper, taskmaster, and self-assessor. Before students began working, the two teachers would dramatize, in an exaggerated, humorous fashion, the appropriate behavior for each role. Ms. Frost was hilarious when she pretended to be a taskmaster who turned into a dictator: "Hey, you! Get to work. Quit being lazy. Do my work for me, too. I rule." The students cracked up. Ms. Savory would then model proper conduct for a taskmaster, again in an exaggerated manner: "Now, now. I think we are getting off task. Let's look at our goals again and be clear about what to do next." Even this positive modeling caused some chuckling from the students, but they got the idea, and it had its desired effect.

▶ **Seatwork and Teacher-Led Activities**

Even though group work, particularly cooperative group work, is a necessary and common practice in elementary and secondary class-rooms, seatwork and teacher-led activities are still a staple of K–12 education (Carnine & Kameenui, 1992; Doyle, 1990; Good & Brophy, 1994). Sometimes direct, whole-class instruction is the best way to provide input for students, and sometimes students must work at their seats practicing and reviewing the content that has been addressed (Anderson, Reder, & Simon, 1995, 1996). To illustrate, in their discussion of cooperative learning, Thomas Good and Jere Brophy (2003) state,

> We recommend cooperative learning methods, although . . . it is important to view cooperative learning not as a wholesale replacement of traditional whole-class instruction, but as an adaptation in which active whole-class instruction is retained but many follow-up activities are accomplished through small-group cooperation rather than through individual seatwork. (p. 288)

Seatwork and teacher-led activities usually involve the expectation that students will remain in their seats. Rules and procedures at the elementary level that pertain to seatwork and teacher-led activities commonly address the following areas:

- Student attention during presentations
- Student participation
- Talking among students
- Obtaining help
- Out-of-seat behavior
- Behavior when work has been completed (see Evertson et al., 2003; Doyle, 1986; Brophy, 1996; Good & Brophy, 2003)

The following vignette depicts how one elementary teacher addressed this area:

Ms. Somerset was masterful at providing appropriate help for students when they worked at their desks. However, this year, for some reason, her procedures were not working. Students not only seemed particularly needy, but also when they raised their hands and did not receive immediate help, they began waving, moaning, and getting out of their seats. Ms. Somerset finally came up with a new color-code system. Each student was given a green, yellow, and red card. When working independently, students were asked to place the green card on their desks to indicate they were getting started. If they began to have problems, they were to place the yellow card on their desk but continue to work on the assignment as best they could until Ms. Somerset could help them. Sometimes students solved their problem on their own before Ms. Somerset got over to them. If this happened, they simply switched back to their green card. This earned them compliments and high-fives from Ms. Somerset. If they were completely stuck and could not continue working at all, students knew that they should place the red card on their desk and read a book quietly until Ms. Somerset could get to them. This color system became a regular part of Ms. Somerset's approach to seatwork.

Rules and procedures at the secondary level that pertain to seatwork and teacher-led activities commonly address the following areas:

- Student attention during presentations
- Student participation
- Talking among students
- Obtaining help
- Out-of-seat behavior
- Behavior when work has been completed (see Emmer et al., 2003; Doyle, 1986; Brophy, 1996; Good & Brophy, 2003)

To understand how these areas might be addressed at the secondary level, consider the following vignette:

In his Advanced Placement Social Studies class, Mr. Wimple had very few rules because he felt that he really didn't need many. Students generally behaved appropriately during teacher-led activities, group work, and seatwork. The only problem he noticed was that some students did the bulk of the talking during group discussions. He had no desire to stifle their enthusiasm, but he wanted some of the more reticent students to speak. To this end, he started discussions by giving each student a certain number of poker chips, the number determined by the length of the discussion time. Before students could speak, they had to toss one of the chips into a box in the middle of the room. When students were out of chips, they had to listen. If students still had all three chips when the discussion was beginning to wind down, Mr. Wimple would elicit ideas from them directly. The result was that more students participated, and the regular participants considered their contributions more carefully before spending a chip.

ACTION STEP 2 ▼

Involve students in the design of rules and procedures.

The second action step you should take relative to classroom rules and procedures is to involve students in their design. As mentioned in the research and theory section of this chapter, the most effective classroom managers don't simply impose rules and procedures on students; rather, they engage students in the design of the rules and procedures.

Before addressing specific rules and procedures with students, it is useful to have a discussion regarding the fact that many situations in real life involve rules and procedures. For example, most students have a sense that there are certain expectations for behavior during dinner when guests are at the house that are different from the rules and procedures that apply when only family members are having dinner together. Similarly, most students are aware of the fact that there are rules and procedures governing behavior in church that do not apply to the behavior in one's own living room. A discussion regarding the importance of rules and procedures in situations outside of school provides a nice set-up for the discussion of classroom rules and procedures.

Next, you might present students with the rules and procedures you have already identified, explaining and providing examples of each one. Students might then discuss those rules and procedures and be invited to suggest alternatives, additions, and deletions. If they disagree on the importance or the specifics of a given rule or procedure, adequate time should be spent addressing the issue. Ideally, a group discussion will produce a compromise rule or procedure that all can live with. If not, you, the teacher, should have the final word in the deliberations. However, the fact that a discussion has taken place will communicate to students that you are concerned about their perceptions and their input. To illustrate how such a discussion might play out in the classroom, consider the following vignette:

On the first day of class, Mr. Whiteside hung large sheets of paper around the room, each with one of the seven important classroom rules printed across the top. Working in groups, students were given seven sticky notes on which they were to write their reaction to each rule and then place it on the corresponding large sheet of paper. They could recommend that the rule remain as presented, or they could make specific suggestions for how the rule might be modified or even eliminated. After all groups had finished, Mr. Whiteside stood next to each rule and read the reaction note from each group. When the notes suggested general agreement, he responded with a promise to consider the recommendations. When the notes represented very different views, he asked groups to explain their views. After some discussion, Mr. Whiteside said he would consider the different viewpoints expressed. A few days later, Mr. Whiteside presented the class with the revised rules. Some students were pleased; others were still not happy. The rules, however, remained in place, and Mr. Whiteside was ready to begin his unit on Principles of Government.

Summary

Classroom rules and procedures are important, but they may vary from one teacher to another. Rules and procedures typically fall into several categories, including general expectations for behavior, beginning and ending the day or the period, transitions and interruptions, materials and equipment, group work, and teacher-led activities. In all cases, it is important to involve students in the design of classroom rules and procedures.

3
DISCIPLINARY INTERVENTIONS

It is probably an understatement to say that discipline is on the minds of many teachers. As noted by J. Ron Nelson, Ron Martella, and Benita Galand (1998), the annual Gallup poll of the public's attitude toward public schools consistently identifies the lack of discipline as the most serious problem facing schools today. Although the research by Gallup addresses discipline at the school level, it is the individual classroom teacher who is the first line of defense for discipline problems. One very disturbing finding from the research is that teachers generally believe that they are not only unprepared to deal with disruptive behavior, but the amount of disruptive behavior in their classes substantially interferes with their teaching (Furlong, Morrison, & Dear, 1994; Lowry, Sleet, Duncan, Powell, & Kolbe, 1995). Cotton (1990) has estimated that only about half of all classroom time is used for instruction, and disciplinary problems occupy most of the other half.

Before discussing this further, it is important to point out that addressing discipline problems is not the sole responsibility of the individual classroom teacher. As discussed in Chapter 8, effective discipline is a combination of effective management at the school level and effective management at the classroom level. In this chapter we address the disciplinary interventions an individual classroom teacher can use. In more specific terms, we address the strategies teachers can use when students do not follow the rules and procedures that have been established as described in Chapter 2.

The Research and Theory

Some people appear to believe that disciplinary actions in almost any form are not only ineffective but counterproductive in terms of student behavior and achievement. Alfie Kohn, for example, has articulated this sentiment in a series of works (see Kohn 1993, 1996). His distrust of disciplinary interventions is evident in his comments regarding punishment:

> How do we punish children? Let us count the ways. We incarcerate them: children are sent to their rooms, teenagers are "grounded" and forbidden to leave the house, students are sent to "detention," and all may be forcibly isolated through "time-out" procedures. (1993, p. 165)

Although Kohn and other like-minded individuals make some useful points (see Wlodkowski, 1982) about inappropriate use of disciplinary technique and the overreliance on punishment, the categorical rejection of disciplinary techniques is simply not supported by research. Quite the contrary, the research and theory strongly support a balanced approach that employs a variety of techniques. To illustrate, a meta-analysis by Scott Stage and David Quiroz (1997) included 99 studies, 200 experimental comparisons, and more than 5,000 students. Their overall finding was that, in general, disciplinary interventions resulted in a decrease in disruptive behavior among almost 80 percent of the subjects in the studies they analyzed. Four of the categories of disciplinary behaviors identified by Stage and Quiroz are particularly relevant to the discussion here. They are (1) reinforcement, (2) punishment, (3) no immediate consequences, and (4) combined punishment and reinforcement.

Disciplinary techniques that fall into Stage and Quiroz's category of *reinforcement* involve recognition or reward for positive behavior or for the timely cessation of negative behavior. Practices classified as *punishment* involve some type of negative consequences for inappropriate behavior. As the name implies,

interventions that are classified as *no immediate consequence* do not involve immediate consequences for inappropriate behavior but do involve some type of reminder when an inappropriate behavior appears imminent. For example, the teacher might remind a student who typically acts out at recess that she should remember to keep herself under control. Finally, the category of *combined punishment and reinforcement* involves recognition or reward for appropriate behavior in conjunction with consequences for inappropriate behavior. Figure 3.1 shows the effect sizes for these categories.

At least two rather striking aspects characterize the findings reported in Figure 3.1. First, the interventions that do not include any type of reaction—positive or negative—to student behavior have the lowest effect size: –.64, which, although it is the lowest effect size, is certainly not small. This makes good intuitive sense. Human beings do best in an environment of feedback—in this case feedback to distinguish between appropriate and inappropriate behaviors. This finding is supported by the conclusion reached by Andy Miller, Eamonn Ferguson, and Rachel Simpson (1998) in their review of the research literature: "Clearly, the results of these studies should permit schools to strike . . . a 'healthy balance' between rewards and punishments" (p. 56).

Second, apparently contradicting the position of those who reject any form of punishment as a viable disciplinary activity, the effect size for interventions that use punishment is quite respectable (–.78). A note of caution is appropriate here. These findings should not be interpreted as an indication that any form of punishment is viable. Indeed, in his review of the research, George Bear (1998) strongly warns that the research

Figure 3.1

Findings from Stage and Quiroz Study

Disciplinary Technique	Average Effect Size	Number of Effect Sizes	Percentile Decrease in Disruptions
Punishment and Reinforcement	−.97	12	33
Reinforcement	−.86	101	31
Punishment	−.78	40	28
No Immediate Consequence	−.64	70	24

Source: Data from Stage and Quiroz (1997).

supports the effectiveness of *mild* forms of punishment only.

In all, then, the findings of Stage and Quiroz strongly support the positive impact of disciplinary techniques. In fact, their findings lead Stage and Quiroz (1997) to comment:

> In summary, this meta-analytic study demonstrates that interventions to reduce disruptive behavior work in public schools. . . . We hope that these findings serve to separate the myth that disruptive classroom behavior cannot be effectively managed from the reality that interventions widely used in our schools do, in fact, reduce disruptive behavior. (pp. 361–362)

Building on the findings of Stage and Quiroz, I organized the studies in my meta-analysis into five categories of interventions, all of which include a balance of negative and positive consequences. My findings appear in Figure 3.2, which reports the average effect sizes for the five categories. As described in Chapter 2, the 95 percent confidence intervals

reported in column three provide an estimate of how confident we are that the average effect sizes reported in column two are the "real" effect size we would obtain if we could eliminate all uncontrolled error in studies. By definition, any confidence interval that does not include 0.00 is significant at the .05 level.

These five types of interventions are discussed in depth in the "Action Steps" section of this chapter. Briefly, though, *teacher reaction* includes the verbal and physical behaviors of teachers that indicate to students that their behavior is appropriate or inappropriate. *Tangible recognition* includes those strategies in which students are provided with some symbol or token for appropriate behavior. These tokens can be used to reward or recognize appropriate behavior. When the student exhibits inappropriate behavior, tangible recognition might be taken away. *Direct cost* involves those interventions that involve a direct and concrete consequence for misbehavior. *Group contingency* strategies are those in which a specific set of students must reach a certain criterion level of appropriate

Figure 3.2

Effect Sizes for Disciplinary Interventions

Type of Disciplinary Intervention	Average Effect Size	95% Confidence Interval	Number of Subjects	Number of Studies	Percentile Decrease in Disruptions
Teacher Reaction	−.997	(−.907) to (−1.087)	1191	25	34
Tangible Recognition	−.823	(−.669) to (−.977)	672	20	29
Direct Cost	−.569	(−.309) to (−.829)	243	7	21
Group Contingency	−.981	(−.781) to (−1.181)	417	13	34
Home Contingency	−.555	(−.251) to (−.858)	169	3	21

behavior. *Home contingency* strategies are those in which behavior monitoring occurs at a student's home. As Figure 3.2 makes clear, all five types of intervention are associated with a decrease in the number of disruptions.

It also appears that disciplinary procedures have an impact on lessening student misbehavior at all grade levels. As Figure 3.3 shows, the effect of disciplinary interventions grows consistently larger the lower the grade-level interval. This does not mean that disciplinary interventions are ineffective at the high school level. Indeed, an average effect size of −.694 for the high school level translates into a 25-percentile-point decrease in disruptive behavior.

Adding to the compelling meta-analytic evidence that appropriate disciplinary interventions produce positive change in student behavior is the evidence that parents, in fact,

Figure 3.3

Effect Sizes for Disciplinary Interventions at Various Grade Levels

Grade Level	Average Effect Size	95% Confidence Interval	Number of Subjects	Number of Studies	Percentile Decrease in Disruptions
High School	−.694	(−.527) to (−.862)	562	7	25
Middle School/Junior High	−.762	(−.536) to (−.987)	312	10	28
Upper Elementary	−.953	(−.863) to (1.1044)	1926	33	33
Primary	−1.046	(−.884) to (−1.208)	622	18	35

expect teachers to discipline their children. For example, in a survey of secondary-level parents, John Coldron and Pam Boulton (1996) report that "many of the parents expressed a preference for schools to achieve discipline in a way that was fair, firm but not severe" (p. 62).

Studies of student opinions are equally illuminating. For example, a number of studies have investigated the opinions of students regarding the effectiveness of various forms of punishments as well as various forms of rewards (Sharpe, Wheldall, & Merrett, 1987; Hougton, Merrett, & Wheldall, 1988; Caffyn, 1989; Harrop & Williams, 1992; Merrett & Tang, 1994; Miller, Ferguson, & Simpson, 1998). In their study of some 50 elementary students and their parents, Andy Miller, Eamonn Ferguson, and Rachel Simpson (1998) examined and compared the opinions of parents and children regarding school and teacher actions they interpreted as negative consequences for inappropriate student behavior. Figure 3.4 presents a summary of their findings. Although their study was conducted in British schools, it is reasonable to assume that U.S. students and British students differ little on this issue.

Figure 3.4
How Parents and Students Rank Negative Consequences

Negative Consequence	Parent Rank	Student Rank	Average Rank
Parents informed about disruptive behavior	1	2	1.5
Student sent to principal	2	5	3.5
Teacher explaining privately what was wrong	3	6	4.5
Teacher confronting student publicly	4	4	4.0
Teacher confronting student privately	5	8	6.5
Student kept in at playtime	6	9	7.5
Teacher explaining what is wrong in front of class	7	3	5.0
Student held back from going on a school trip	8	1	4.5
Student moved to another seat in the classroom	9	10	9.5
Student took unfinished work to another classroom	10	7	8.5

Source: Adapted from Andy Miller, Eamonn Ferguson, and Rachel Simpson, The perceived effectiveness of rewards and sanctions in primary schools: Adding in the parental perspective, *Educational Psychology, 18*(1), 55–64. Copyright © 1998 Taylor & Francis Ltd., http://www.tandf.co.uk/journals

The results in Figure 3.4 provide an interesting comparison with those depicted in Figure 3.5, which reports parent and student ratings of actions considered as positive consequences for acceptable behavior. Note that in Figure 3.4, parents rank being informed about student misbehavior in school as the most effective negative consequence, and students rank this action second. The same pattern is found in Figure 3.5. Parents rank being informed about positive student behavior first, and students rank it second. From this study, it appears that communication with the home can be used as both a powerful negative consequence and a powerful positive consequence.

An interesting perspective on student opinions about discipline emerged from a study conducted by Patricia Kearney, Timothy Plax, Ellis Hays, and Marilyn Ivey (1991). They asked college students about the misbehavior of *teachers*. Specifically they asked students to describe behaviors of their teachers that they considered inappropriate. In all, 254 students generated 1,762 examples of specific instances of inappropriate teacher behaviors they had actually witnessed. The list included the following:

- Absenteeism
- Tardiness

Figure 3.5
How Parents and Students Rank Positive Consequences

Positive Consequence	Parent Rank	Student Rank	Average Rank
Parents informed about good behavior	1	2	1.5
Student receives good marks	2	1	1.5
Student receives good written comments on work	3	3	3.0
Student praised in front of other students	4	6	5.0
Student mentioned in assembly	5	4	4.5
Student's work displayed	6	5	5.5
Student praised privately	7	9	8.0
Student praised by other pupils	8	7	7.5
Whole class praised	9	8	8.5

Source: Adapted from Andy Miller, Eamonn Ferguson, and Rachel Simpson, The perceived effectiveness of rewards and sanctions in primary schools: Adding in the parental perspective, *Educational Psychology, 18*(1), 55–64. Copyright © 1998 Taylor & Francis Ltd., http://www.tandf.co.uk/journals

- Keeping students overtime
- Early dismissal
- Straying from the subject matter
- Being unprepared or unorganized
- Being late returning work
- Sarcasm and put-downs
- Verbal abuse
- Unreasonable and arbitrary rules
- Lack of response to student questions
- Sexual harassment
- Apathy toward students
- Unfair grading practices
- Negative personality
- Showing favoritism

One of the clear messages from this study is that students have a strong sense of "fairness" when it comes to behavioral expectations. If they feel that teachers are behaving inappropriately, they will resist efforts to monitor their behavior. Again, it should be noted that this study surveyed college students, but it is reasonable to assume that the findings would generalize at least to high school students.

Finally, some research indicates that the higher the grade level, the more disciplinary problems occur in public schools (McFadden, Marsch, Price, & Hwang, 1992). This may be due to several factors such as peer influences, environmental influences, gender differences, and emotional and behavioral difficulties due to puberty (Fry & Gabriel, 1994; Sanson, Prior, Smart, & Oberklaid, 1993; Zoccolillo, 1993).

Programs

This section describes only two of a number of programs that emphasize disciplinary techniques: Think Time and Assertive Discipline.

(For reviews of other effective schoolwide programs, see Brophy, 1996; Nelson, Martella, & Galand, 1998; Bear, 1998.)

Think Time (Nelson & Carr, 1999) is a highly structured program that has been shown to decrease disruptive behavior in students as well as increase student engagement (see Sugai & Colvin, 1996 for a review of the research). It has three basic goals:

- To provide for consistent consequences across all teachers in the school when students engage in disruptive behavior
- To provide students with feedback for their disruptive behavior and to allow for planning to avoid future incidents of such behavior
- To enable teachers and students to cut off negative social exchanges and initiate positive ones

We will consider the Think Time program in more depth in Chapter 8 when we address the adoption of a schoolwide program. Briefly though, one of the defining features of Think Time is the "Think Time classroom"— a dedicated room where students are sent when teachers cannot successfully address a disruptive behavior in the context of the regular classroom. A symbiotic relationship links the Think Time classroom and the regular classroom. Teachers follow specific procedures for addressing inappropriate or disruptive behavior and make every attempt to do so in the context of the regular classroom. However, if students cannot or will not respond to efforts in the regular classroom, they are sent to the Think Time classroom, where they are expected to analyze and think seriously about their behavior. They do not return to the regular classroom until they demonstrate that they are aware of the behavior that led to their assignment to the Think Time classroom, understand appropriate alternative behaviors, and are willing to adopt those alternative behaviors.

Assertive Discipline (Canter & Canter, 1976) is a widely used program based originally on traditional behavior modification approaches in which misbehavior results in specific consequences. Because of this, some have referred to it as being grounded in "interventionist" ideology (Wolfgang, 1995; Charles, 1996). Some have criticized the program rather harshly. For example, in his book *Punished by Rewards: The Trouble with Gold Stars, Incentive Plans, A's, Praise, and Other Bribes*, Kohn (1993) expresses the opinion that Assertive Discipline is fundamentally flawed. He also notes, "Even if it did succeed in keeping order in the classroom, this program, like all carrot-and-stick techniques used at school or at home, fails to help children become reflective, compassionate people" (p. 165).

Other researchers do not share Kohn's negative opinion and believe that a careful analysis of the research on the program leads to a different conclusion (see Brophy, 1996). In fact, Kohn's objections are directed to the original version of Assertive Discipline. Since its inception, the program has changed rather dramatically (see Canter and Canter, 1992). First, it makes a sharper distinction between rules and directions. Rules are generally in effect all the time, whereas directions vary from activity to activity. Second, students' off-task *disruptive* behavior is distinguished from their off-task *nondisruptive* behavior. If a student is off-task but not disrupting anyone, the teacher redirects the off-task behavior but

imposes no consequences. Third, the current version emphasizes positive consequences for appropriate behavior, whereas the original version placed more emphasis on negative consequences for inappropriate behavior. Fourth, negative consequences are kept to a minimum—the emphasis is on consistency as opposed to severity of consequences. Fifth, tracking of behavior is a private matter as opposed to a public matter, which was a prominent feature in the original version.

Implementing the current version of Assertive Discipline involves five steps. The first step focuses on establishing a positive climate for discipline. This requires teachers to replace negative expectations of students with positive ones. The second step is for teachers to learn about and practice assertive behavior. Specifically, teachers learn the difference between assertive, nonassertive, and hostile behavior. Ideally, teachers practice assertive behavior until it becomes habitual. In general, assertive teacher responses convey disapproval in a firm, unemotional, businesslike manner and include a communication of expected behavior. The third step is to establish limits and consequences. To signal students that they are approaching a limit, teachers give hints to alert students, ask questions, and occasionally make demands. The fourth step is following through on consequences if a student has exceeded the limits. The final step is to implement a system of rewards or positive consequences for positive behavior. These changes in Assertive Discipline are substantive and have transformed it into a program that employs a balance of negative and positive consequences as opposed to negative consequences only, as is commonly thought.

ActionSteps

ACTION STEP 1 ▼

Employ specific techniques that acknowledge and reinforce acceptable behavior and acknowledge and provide negative consequences for unacceptable behavior.

As discussed earlier, my meta-analysis identified five categories of disciplinary interventions that can be used to provide a balance of positive and negative consequences: teacher reaction, tangible recognition, direct cost, group contingency, and home contingency. This action step applies to all five categories.

▶ Teacher Reaction

Verbal and physical teacher reactions are the simplest ways to acknowledge and reinforce acceptable behavior and to acknowledge and provide negative consequences for unacceptable behavior. Emmer, Evertson, and Worsham (2003) list a variety of teacher reactions that include the following:

• Make eye contact with an offending student by moving closer to her. This is a subtle but powerful way of alerting a student to the fact that she is misbehaving.
• Use a physical signal such as a finger to the lips or shake of the head to indicate that a given action is inappropriate.
• If a student is not following a procedure, provide the student with a simple verbal reminder—ideally as privately and subtly

as possible. You might also state the expected appropriate behavior.
• If a student is simply "off task" but not misbehaving, simply state the desired appropriate behavior.
• If a student does not respond to the more subtle interventions, simply tell the student to stop the inappropriate behavior.

Though simple, these practices have been shown to decrease student misbehavior (Madsen, Becker, & Thomas, 1968).

Stimulus cueing is another teacher reaction strategy. It involves providing a cue to students before inappropriate behavior occurs (Carr & Durand, 1985; Lobitz, 1974). For example, a teacher might determine that a specific student usually starts talking to other students around him before he engages in more severe disruptive behavior. With this prior condition identified and communicated to the student, the teacher might place a mark on a notepad that is kept open on the student's desk every time the student begins talking to others around him, thus providing a private cue to the student that he is about to engage in an activity that will probably result in negative consequences for him.

The examples above all address inappropriate behavior. Teacher reaction is also an effective technique for reinforcing appropriate behavior. In their book *Discipline with Dignity*, Richard Curwin and Allen Mendler (1988) describe a strategy they refer to as "catching a student being good" (p. 97). They explain:

About every 15 to 20 minutes (2 or 3 times in a secondary class), catch a student being good . . . speak softly so no other student can hear. Tell the student you like the way he is paying attention, or that he did a nice job on his homework because it was very detailed, or that the questions he is asking in class are very thought provoking . . . This strategy helps ensure the students' privacy because other students will never know if your private discussion was positive feedback or giving a consequence. The student might make the conversation public, but then it becomes his responsibility to deal with the loss of privacy. (p. 97)

Curwin and Mendler assert that students so look forward to this positive form of teacher reaction that when it is withheld because no examples of "good behavior" are evident, they consider it a subtle form of negative consequence.

In summary, teacher reaction is a straightforward and powerful way to provide both positive and negative consequences for student behavior. The following vignettes illustrate two teacher reaction strategies.

- *Ms. Wood knew her students well. When Colin began to be disruptive during a class discussion, she simply moved over to him and leaned on his desk, without interrupting the class discussion. When he stopped, she moved on. With Shawna, being proactive was more effective. Shawna frequently had to sharpen her pencil and, on the way to the sharpener, tended to annoy other students. Ms. Wood decreased the frequency of this behavior by watching Shawna carefully. The second she took out a sharpened pencil, Ms. Wood walked over and complimented her on being so prepared that she would not have to leave her seat during work time.*
- *Many 8th graders, Mr. Foseid knew, did not like attention drawn to them, not*

even positive attention. He therefore established a more subtle "thumbs up" signal to reinforce positive behavior. His goal was, at least once every class period, to catch a student's eye and give him or her the signal. He knew that students coveted this acknowledgment, and he noticed that doing this made him feel better at the end of the day.

▶ Tangible Recognition

As its name indicates, *tangible recognition* involves the use of some concrete symbol of appropriate behavior. Sometimes approaches in this category are referred to as *token economies* because they frequently involve providing some type of chit for appropriate behavior or the cessation of inappropriate behavior. Students later exchange these tokens for privileges, activities, or items (Reitz, 1994). At first, the research on token economies was focused on improving positive behaviors only (O'Leary, Becker, Evans, & Saudargas, 1969). However, research has demonstrated that tokens are most effective if awarded for positive behaviors and taken away for negative behaviors (Kaufman & O'Leary, 1972).

As defined here, tangible recognition involves any type of concrete recognition or reward provided by the teacher. It is important to note that any system of tangible recognition should be accompanied by a thorough discussion of the rationale behind the system. Additionally, care should be taken to ensure that tangible recognition is not perceived or used as some type of bribe or form of coercion relative to student behavior. This is perhaps Kohn's biggest objection to these systems— and rightfully so (Kohn, 1993, 1996). The following vignette describes one teacher's approach to tangible recognition.

At the beginning of class, Mr. Powell had his students fill out the following goal sheet:

Date	Goals for Today	Self-Assessment	On-Task
	1. _____	1. _____	
	2. _____	2. _____	
	3. _____	3. _____	

In the "On-Task" cell, the students awarded themselves 5 points. These points were recorded in the grade book as part of students' participation grade, but students also accumulated them to trade for Jolly Ranchers on a designated day each month. (Mr. Powell was surprised that some students really wanted those points for "Jolly Rancher Days.") During class, if a student exhibited off-task behavior, Mr. Powell simply walked over and crossed out the 5 and replaced it with a 4. As soon as he noticed that the student was back on task and was staying on task, he changed the 4 back to a 5. Because he believed that in most cases students knew exactly why he was adding or subtracting points, he said nothing to them unless absolutely necessary. He found that, using this system, all his verbal interactions with students were focused on the positive aspects of their behavior as opposed to the negative aspects.

▶ **Direct Cost**

As described here, direct-cost techniques are more oriented toward negative consequences than positive consequences for student behavior. As the name implies, these strategies involve an explicit and direct consequence for inappropriate student behavior. One powerful direct cost strategy is isolation time out.

Isolation time out refers to the removal of a student from the classroom to a location reserved for disruptive students. Although this strategy was originally designed to be used in special education settings for students with severe behavior disorders (see Drabman & Spitalnik, 1973), it has been used quite successfully in regular education settings (Zabel, 1986). However, it should be noted that teachers may easily abuse isolation time out if they simply wish to "get rid of" a behavioral problem as opposed to addressing it (Harris, 1985).

The effective use of isolation time out requires that students have a clear understanding as to the specific behaviors that will lead to its use. Additionally, students should be aware that isolation time out would be used only when other attempts to correct disruptive behavior within the regular context of the classroom have been exhausted. The following vignette depicts how one teacher used isolation time out.

When a behavior problem could not be solved in the classroom, students at Main Middle School were often sent for "time out" to a small room adjacent to the assistant principal's office. The assistant principal often interacted with students sent for time out, and he became the one who followed through with disciplinary actions. Ms. Canyon, however, wanted the room to be used as it was intended, as a time-out room where offending students were isolated from others. She requested that, when she sent students to the room, no one was to interact with them. "I will be down as soon as possible to address the issue, but I want the student to have no *interactions. It is important that I be the person who follows through, one-on-one with the student. That is the only way I can address the root cause of the problem and maintain the right relationship with the student."* The assistant principal was understandably grateful for this approach.

Overcorrection is a procedure that is used when a student has misbehaved in a way that destroys or alters some physical aspect of the classroom. For example, if a student's misbehavior results in an overturned desk, then an overcorrection intervention would require the student not only to right the overturned desk, but also to straighten out the classroom. That is, the student would be asked to overcompensate for the behavior, thus sending a powerful message about its consequences (see Foxx, 1978). The following vignette depicts how overcorrection might be used.

> *Terrell was not happy about having to sit and repair all of the torn pages in the dictionaries in his classroom. Unfortunately, he had lost his temper in class the day before and damaged the dictionary he had been using. Further, this was not the first time he had damaged books in his possession. His teacher, therefore, scheduled several after-school sessions during which Terrell repaired books by taping torn pages and erasing stray marks. She also used this quiet, focused time to try to connect with Terrell and chat with him about ways to redirect his temper.*

▶ Group Contingency

Group contingency techniques operate in a fashion similar to concrete recognition techniques except that they apply to a pre-established group of students as opposed to individuals. For example, you might establish some type of reward if the entire class remembers to raise

their hands before speaking out for an entire class period, or if they forget to raise their hands only a set number of times for the entire day. Researchers and theorists commonly distinguish between interdependent group contingency techniques and dependent group contingency techniques (Litow & Pumroy, 1975). *Interdependent group contingency* techniques require every student in the group to meet the behavioral criterion for the group to earn credit. The previous example illustrates an interdependent group contingency technique because the target behavior of raising their hands before speaking out applies to all students. *Dependent group contingency* techniques require a specific individual or a specific set of individuals in the group to meet the behavioral criterion for the group to earn credit. In the previous example, dependent group contingency would apply if one or a few students in the class were singled out for their hand-raising behavior but the entire class received the concrete recognition.

Obviously, the dependent group contingency strategy places a great deal of peer pressure on those who have been singled out. In fact, this appears to be one reason why it works. However, some teachers rightly are concerned that this approach could embarrass the identified students. Consequently, I recommend that teachers use dependent group contingency techniques with caution. The following vignette depicts one use of group contingency.

> *Ms. Muldoon likes the students in her class to work together, to feel a sense of community. "We sink or swim together," she often reminds them. From the very beginning of the year, she sets up behavior expectations that, if followed by every student, result in the class receiving Pressure Points. For example, if every student follows the procedures for putting materials*

away after math, the entire class earns 25 Pressure Points. The class can then use these points to negotiate with Ms. Muldoon about—to "pressure" her into—postponing a test, scheduling a "no homework" night, or allowing extra time for a big project. Not only does the class earn the points as a group, this plan also forces them to come to consensus about how to spend the points.

▶ **Home Contingency**

As described in the section of this chapter on research and theory, home contact can be a powerful form of positive and negative consequence. In its most basic form, home contingency simply involves making parents aware of the positive and negative behaviors of their children. This might occur in the form of a short note or letter to parents, a phone call, or a visit. Some teachers have developed preprinted notes with space where they can add comments. These forms are used to signify both negative and positive behavior.

At a more detailed level, you might establish a system of positive and negative consequences to be enacted at home. This usually requires face-to-face meetings with parents to establish the specifics of these consequences. (We will consider the dynamics of these meetings in Chapters 4 and 6.) For example, you might meet with the parents of a given student to discuss the specific classroom behavior that will be targeted. Together, you and the student's parents would identify positive and negative consequences for the student's appropriate and inappropriate behavior, respectively. With these parameters established, you would then keep track of the student's behavior and systematically report to parents so that they might enact the positive and negative consequences. The following

vignette describes how one teacher used home contingency.

Karla and Keisha were popular twins in their class. However, they earned much of their popularity by being "class clowns," often making it difficult for Mr. Beatty to keep the class on task. This behavior was particularly disruptive when Karla and Keisha seemed to be competing to determine who could be the biggest clown. After exhausting many disciplinary approaches, Mr. Beatty contacted the twins' parents, who were obviously aware that the girls could exhibit these behaviors, but who were also not sure what they could do. As a result of problem solving together, the parents and Mr. Beatty agreed that he would call the home every Friday afternoon to report on the twins' behavior. If both girls had been on task and behaving appropriately all week, they were allowed to rent movies on Friday night, something they loved to do. However, a bad report meant not only no movies, but also no television or computer time—nothing on a screen. Mr. Beatty saw results in the first week.

ACTION STEP 2 ▼

Establish clear limits for unacceptable behavior and an effective system to record these behaviors.

To use positive and negative consequences effectively, you must establish limits. For example, assume that you are working on decreasing the number of times students talk without first raising their hands using a group contingency approach. It would be unrealistic to expect all students to remember to raise their hands every time they want to speak. With the students' input and discussion, you would identify a number of "slips in proto-col" that would be considered acceptable during a specific time interval—let's say a class period. If the number of infractions were below this criterion number, students would receive some type of concrete recognition. If the number of infractions were above the limit, none would be provided.

Setting limits is a perfect opportunity to involve students in their own management. Rather than you establishing the limits in isolation, the class could do so after discussing why the target behavior is important and what are fair expectations regarding that behavior. The limit established by a consensus approach would be the limit used by you, the teacher. The following vignette depicts one teacher's approach to limits.

> *Mrs. Campbell explained to her students that she had a "no candy and gum" rule because she was trying to support the custodial staff, who hated spending time removing sticky gum and candy from school furniture and rugs. Her class understood but also argued that there should be some leeway before detention was given, especially during holiday season when so much candy was around. Ms. Campbell finally agreed that the first time students were caught with candy or gum, they would receive a warning; the second time, they would receive after-school detention; and the third time, students would have to stay after school and help custodians clean up the school.*

Once limits are established, you need a good record-keeping procedure to keep track of student behavior (Deitz & Repp, 1973; Irvin & Lundervold, 1988). In general, the simpler the record-keeping format, the better. The original version of the Assertive Discipline program (Canter & Canter, 1976) used a very detailed and public form of record keeping involving check marks on a white board. Less dramatic forms of record keeping are more common now, such as the teacher or student—or both—keeping the record privately. This is not to say that public record keeping is ineffective. If done appropriately, it can work well. However, with highly public record-keeping schemes you run the risk of diverting attention from the behavior to the record keeping. The following is an example of one teacher's record-keeping scheme.

> *Mrs. Babbage was expert at using her PalmPilot to keep extensive student records. Not only could she record grades and anecdotal information, she had a coding system that used small icons and tally marks for keeping track of students' behaviors, both positive and negative. When students worked hard, for example, and participated enthusiastically, or, conversely, did little and were disruptive, she could quickly record that behavior in the student's personal record. At any time, she could show students their personal screen and quietly compliment or caution them, as appropriate.*

Summary

The guiding principle for disciplinary interventions is that they should include a healthy balance between negative consequences for inappropriate behavior and positive consequences for appropriate behavior. Specific techniques that involve both positive and negative consequences include teacher reaction, tangible recognition, direct cost, group contingency, and home contingency. Whatever the approach, it is important to establish behavioral limits and a record-keeping system that allows you to keep track of student behavior efficiently and unobtrusively.

4

TEACHER–STUDENT RELATIONSHIPS

The third aspect of effective classroom management, after rules and procedures and disciplinary interventions, is teacher-student relationships. One might make the case that teacher-student relationships are the keystone for the other factors. If a teacher has a good relationship with students, then students more readily accept the rules and procedures and the disciplinary actions that follow their violations. Without the foundation of a good relationship, students commonly resist rules and procedures along with the consequent disciplinary actions. Again, this makes good intuitive sense.

The Research and Theory

The results of my meta-analysis for teacher-student relationships are reported in Figure 4.1. What is perhaps most striking about the findings is not the average effect size of –.869

(which is sizable and impressive in itself), but the extremely large effect sizes for the middle school/junior high level and the upper elementary level. (Note that data were not available to compute an average effect size for the primary level.) I should caution that if more studies of the impact of teacher-student relationships on student behavior were available, these large average effect sizes would probably go down. They are simply much larger than are commonly found in the social sciences. Nevertheless, it makes sense that teacher-student relationships would be extremely important to students below the high school level and, therefore, would have a profound impact on student behavior.

Along with the meta-analytic evidence of the importance of teacher-student relationships is the more perceptual evidence. To illustrate, in a study involving 68 high school students, 84 percent said that disciplinary

Figure 4.1
Effect Sizes for Teacher-Student Relationships

	Average Effect Size	95% Confidence Interval	Number of Subjects	Number of Studies	Percentile Decrease in Disruptions
Teacher-Student Relationship	−.869	(−.743) to (−.995)	1,100	4	31
High School	−.549	(−.338) to (−.760)	720	2	21
Middle School/Junior High	−2.891	(−1.786) to (−4.008)	350	1	50
Upper Elementary	−1.606	(−1.364) to (−1.849)	350	1	45

Note: Data were not available to compute an effect size for the primary level.

problems that occurred could have been avoided by better teacher-student relationships (Sheets, 1994). In their review of the literature, Rosa Sheets and Geneva Gay (1996) note that many behavioral problems ultimately boil down to a breakdown in teacher-student relationships: "The causes of many classroom behaviors labeled and punished as rule infractions are, in fact, problems of students and teachers relating to each other interpersonally" (pp. 86–87). Some researchers have postulated that this breakdown occurs because many teachers position themselves in a "we-they" relationship with students (Plax & Kearney, 1990).

Researchers have tried repeatedly to identify general characteristics of teachers that make them more likable to students and, consequently, more likely to have good relationships with students (e.g., Barr, 1958; Good & Brophy, 1995). These studies identify characteristics such as consideration, buoyancy, patience, and the like, but they do not focus on the dynamics of the teacher-student relationship per se. However, a number of studies have focused either directly or indirectly on this dynamic.

In terms of classroom management techniques, one of the most useful efforts to identify the dynamics of an effective teacher-student relationship is the work of Theo Wubbels and his colleagues (see Wubbels, Brekelmans, van Tartwijk, & Admiral, 1999; Wubbels & Levy, 1993; Brekelmans, Wubbels, & Creton, 1990). Building on the early work of Timothy Leary (1957), Wubbels and his colleagues (see Wubbels & Levy, 1993; Wubbels et al., 1999) identify two dimensions whose interactions define the relationship between teacher and students. One dimension is dominance versus submission; the other is cooperation versus opposition.

High dominance is characterized by clarity of purpose and strong guidance. The purpose and guidance provided by the teacher should be both academic and behavioral—that is, the teacher provides purpose and guidance relative to the content addressed in class as well as the behavior expected in class. These are certainly positive characteristics.

However, high dominance can also be characterized by lack of attentiveness to and concern for the interests of students. The other end of this continuum—high submission—is characterized by lack of clarity and purpose. Neither end point of the continuum—extreme dominance or extreme submission—defines an optimal teacher-student relationship. This is also the case with the second dimension—cooperation versus opposition.

High cooperation is characterized by a concern for the needs and opinions of others and a desire to function as a member of a team as opposed to an individual. Again, these are positive traits. But extreme cooperation is characterized by an inability or lack of resolve to act without the input and approval

of others. Extreme opposition—the other end of this continuum—is characterized by active antagonism toward others and a desire to thwart their goals and desires. Again, neither end point—extreme cooperation or extreme opposition—can be characterized as the type of teacher-student relationship conducive to learning. It is the right combination of moderate to high dominance (as opposed to extreme dominance) and moderate to high cooperation (as opposed to extreme cooperation) that provides the optimal teacher-student relationship for learning. Figure 4.2 illustrates this relationship.

The shaded area in Figure 4.2 depicts the optimal teacher-student relationship profile in terms of dominance and cooperation. Again,

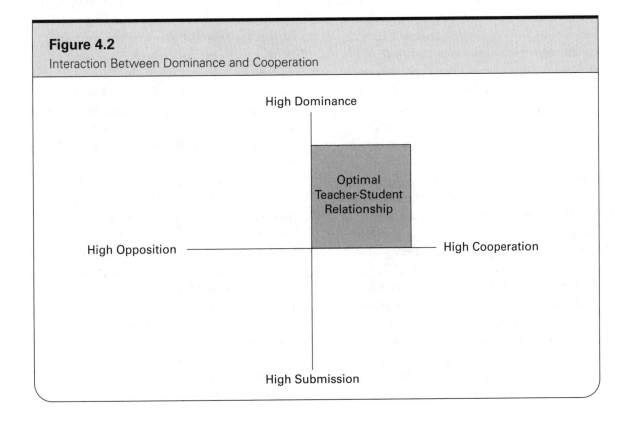

Figure 4.2
Interaction Between Dominance and Cooperation

High Dominance

Optimal Teacher-Student Relationship

High Opposition —— —— High Cooperation

High Submission

notice that this area does not include extreme levels of dominance or cooperation. As Wubbels and his colleagues (1999) note:

> Briefly, teachers should be effective instructors and lecturers, as well as friendly, helpful, and congenial. They should be able to empathize with students, understand their world, and listen to them. Good teachers are not uncertain, undecided, or confusing in the way they communicate with students. They are not grouchy, gloomy, dissatisfied, aggressive, sarcastic, or quick-tempered. They should be able to set standards and maintain control while still allowing students responsibility and freedom to learn. (p. 167)

Interestingly, when teachers first enter the profession, they more readily exhibit behaviors that would be characterized as highly cooperative. However, given their lack of experience in leadership positions, they are not very good at exhibiting behaviors that are highly dominant (Wubbels & Levy, 1993). Over time (between 6 and 10 years), they become quite competent at dominant behaviors. Unfortunately, they also become less cooperative. As Wubbels and his colleagues put it: "Teachers appear to decline in cooperative behavior and increase in oppositional behavior, a change that negatively affects student attitudes" (Wubbels et al., 1999, p. 166).

Lian Chiu and Michael Tulley (1997) conducted a study that supports the conclusions of Wubbels and his colleagues. They interviewed 712 students in grades 4, 5, and 6 (368 males and 344 females). The students were presented with four options in terms of their preferences for the management style of teachers: (1) rules/rewards-punishments,

(2) relationship-listening, (3) confronting-contracting, and (4) no preferred approach. The first three approaches were based on a description of classroom management styles articulated by Wolfgang and Glickman (1986). The *rules/rewards-punishments* style is described well by its title. Teachers using this style articulate rules and procedures and present them to students. Acting in accordance with the rules results in positive consequences; not acting in accordance with the rules results in negative consequences. The *relationship-listening* style is characterized by little or no emphasis on disciplinary issues per se. Rather, the emphasis is on attending to student concerns. Finally, the *confronting-contracting* style is characterized by direct attention to disciplinary problems but not in an inflexible way. Along with executing negative consequences for inappropriate behavior, the teacher demonstrates a concern for students' needs and preferences. The responses of students are summarized in Figure 4.3.

The data in Figure 4.3 confirm students' clear preference for the confronting-contracting style. The percentage of students who preferred the confronting-contracting approach is at least double that for any other approach. One might say that confronting-contracting by another name is the confluence of appropriate dominance with appropriate cooperation as defined by Wubbels.

A study by Jere Brophy and Carolyn Evertson (1976) also supports the importance of a combination of teacher dominance and cooperation. They examined the practices of some 30 second and third grade teachers who had consistently produced achievement gains greater than expected as compared to a group of randomly selected comparison teachers. Among other things, they noted:

Figure 4.3

Student Preferences for Management Types

Grade	Gender	Rules/ Reward- Punishment	Listening	Confront/ Contract	No Preference	Total
4	M	22 (20%)	16 (15%)	67 (62%)	3 (3%)	108
4	F	24 (27%)	16 (18%)	47 (53%)	2 (2%)	89
5	M	16 (14%)	27 (24%)	65 (57%)	6 (5%)	114
5	F	9 (10%)	18 (20%)	59 (64%)	6 (7%)	92
6	M	21 (14%)	34 (23%)	80 (55%)	11 (8%)	146
6	F	29 (18%)	24 (15%)	102 (63%)	8 (5%)	163
Total		121 (17%)	135 (19%)	420 (59%)	36 (5%)	712

Source: Adapted with permission from Lian Hwang Chiu and Micheal Tulley, Student preferences of teacher discipline styles, *Journal of Instructional Psychology, 24*(3), 169–175. Copyright 1997.

Teachers who felt a sense of inner control and took personal responsibility for what went on in their classrooms showed that *they were in charge* [original emphasis]. They designed and maintained the general learning environment of the classroom. Although they often solicited or accepted suggestions from the children, they retained control over what went on, how it went on, and when it went on. These teachers also tended to be the ones who were the most successful in obtaining student learning gains. (p. 42)

The final conclusions of Brophy and Evertson are basically the same as those reached by Wubbels. An optimal teacher-student relationship consists of equal parts of dominance and cooperation.

A final line of research that provides a useful perspective on the nature of an effective teacher-student relationship is one that addresses the needs of different types of students. Public school teachers must deal with all of America's children with the exception of incarcerated teens and children and teens in mental hospitals. These students enter the classroom with a staggering array of serious issues in their lives. Figure 4.4 provides a brief summary of some types of problems students face in their lives and, consequently, the types of issues teachers must deal with.

The research findings reported in Figure 4.4 are sobering indeed. The more general descriptions of problems facing students are equally sobering. In their review of the research on child mistreatment, Ross Thompson and Jennifer Wyatt (1999) note that a high

Figure 4.4

Categories of Severe Problems Facing Students

Category	Statistics
Homelessness	On any given night, 700,000 people are homeless. Two million people are homeless annually. Twelve million people are homeless at some point in their lives. Forty percent of the homeless have homeless children. *(National Center on Homelessness and Poverty, in Crespi, 2001)*
Depression	About 8 percent of all adolescents are depressed in any given year. *(U.S. Department of Health and Human Services [1999], in Stanard, 2000)* Five percent of youth between 9 and 17 years old are depressed, and only a minority of youth are treated. *(Shaffer [1998] in Stanard, 2000)*
Suicide	Among youth 15 to 19 years old, suicide is responsible for more deaths than any disease. For 10- to 14-year-olds, suicide is the 4th leading cause of death. *(Centers for Disease Control [2000] in Stanard, 2000)*
Violent Students	A majority of violent and aggressive students who have been suspended or expelled have identifiable substance abuse or mental health disorders. *(Office of Juvenile Justice and Delinquency Prevention [1999], in Luongo, 2000)* For more than 56 percent of youth who are victims of violence, the emotional and physical assault occurred on school grounds. *(Porter, Epp, & Bryant, 2000)* More than 50 percent of all boys and 25 percent of all girls report that they have been physically assaulted in school. *(Centers for Disease Control [1992], in Porter, et al., 2000)* Twenty percent of all children and youth, or approximately 11 million, have diagnosable developmental, behavioral, and/or emotional problems that increase their risk of becoming victims and/or perpetrators of violence. *(Porter et al., 2000)*
Eating Disorders	Fifteen to 18 percent of high school students manifest bulimic symptoms. *(Crago, Shisslak, & Estes, 1996)* Five to 10 percent of cases of anorexia nervosa are males. *(Crosscope-Happel, Hutchins, Getz, & Hayes, 2000)*
Alcoholism	Twenty percent of children in the United States grow up in alcoholic families. *(National Institute on Drug Abuse [1998], in Johnson, 2001)* Alcoholic families exhibit greater levels of openly expressed anger and lower levels of warmth, cohesion, and direct communication than nonalcoholic families. *(Johnson, 2001)* Alcohol is a significant factor in approximately 81 percent of child abuse cases. *(Johnson, 2001)*
Attention Deficit and Hyperactivity Disorder	Three to 7 percent of school-age children, mostly males, experience ADHD disorder. *(American Psychiatric Association, 2000)* Approximately 50 percent of the 1.6 million elementary school–aged children with ADHD also have learning disorders. *(Centers for Disease Control [1997–98], in "CDC Study Confirms ADHD/Learning Disability Link," n.d.)*

▶ Continued...

Figure 4.4

Categories of Severe Problems Facing Students *(continued)*

Category	Statistics
Attention Deficit and Hyperactivity Disorder *(cont.)*	The predominantly inattentive subtype of ADHD has a prevalence rate of 3 to 5 percent. *(Erk, 2000)* Nearly 70 percent of those with ADHD simultaneously cope with other conditions such as learning disabilities, mood disorders, anxiety, and more. *(Ross, 2002)*
Sexual Orientation	Six percent of students describe themselves as homosexual or bisexual, and 13 percent are uncertain about their sexual orientation. Homosexual and bisexual students have higher than average rates of mental health problems and eating disorders and are more concerned about sexual victimization. *(Harvard Medical Newsletter, 2000)*
Incarcerated Parents	One and a half million children have an incarcerated parent. Ten million young people have had a mother or father or both behind bars at some point in their lives. *(Kleiner, 2002)*
Poverty	Approximately 15.7 million children live in households with incomes below the poverty line. Almost 50 percent of all children in mother-only families are impoverished. More than 4 million children are latch-key children. *(Herr, 2002)* Fifty percent of urban and rural poor students manifest learning, behavioral, and emotional problems. *(Adelman & Taylor, 2002)*
Sexual and Physical Abuse	In 1993, 1.55 million children were reported as maltreated, and another 1.22 million were in imminent danger, reflecting a near doubling of the abuse rate between 1986 and 1993. *(U.S. Department of Health and Human Services [1996], in Thompson & Wyatt, 1999)* On average, more than 5 children die every day from injuries or prolonged deprivation suffered from their caregivers. *(U.S. Advisory Board on Child Abuse and Neglect [1995] in Thompson & Wyatt, 1999)*

proportion of students referred for behavioral or conduct problems in school have a history of physical or sexual abuse, with some reports estimating that as many as 60 to 70 percent of these students have been abused. In general, between 12 and 22 percent of all children in school suffer from mental, emotional, or behavioral disorders, and relatively few receive mental health services (Adelman & Taylor, 2002). The director of the Center for Demographics Policy estimates that 40 percent of young people are at risk of failure in

school because of serious problems outside of school (Adelman &Taylor, 2002). Finally, the Association of School Counselors notes that 18 percent of students have special needs that require extraordinary intervention and treatment that go beyond the typical resources available to the classroom teacher (Dunn & Baker, 2002).

School may be the only place where the needs of many of these children facing extreme challenges are addressed. Although not usually considered part of the regular job of classroom teachers, addressing these severe issues is unfortunately a reality in today's schools. Jere Brophy examined this issue as part of the Classroom Strategy Study (see Brophy, 1996; Brophy & McCaslin, 1992). The study involved in-depth interviews with and observations of 98 teachers, some of whom were identified as effective managers and some of whom were not. The heart of the study involved presenting teachers with vignettes regarding specific types of students (e.g., hostile-aggressive students, passive-aggressive students, hyperactive students) in specific situations. Among the many findings from the study was that the most effective classroom managers tended to employ different strategies with different types of students, whereas ineffective managers did not. Specifically, effective managers made distinctions about the most appropriate strategies to use with individual students based on the unique needs of those students. Although Brophy does not couch the findings from his study in terms of teacher-student relationships, the link is obvious. Effective managers do not treat all students the same, particularly in situations involving behavior problems. Whereas some students need encouragement, other students need a gentle reprimand, and still others might require a not-so-gentle reprimand. In fact, one strong recommendation by Brophy (1996) is that teachers develop a set of "helping skills" to employ with different types of students.

Programs

Again, no one program focuses specifically on teacher-student relationships. However, one of the most popular staff development programs is very strong in this area. Teacher Expectations and Student Achievement, or TESA (Kerman, Kimball, & Martin, 1980), is a well-established teacher-training program that has been referred to as "one of the most-used offerings in staff development programs across the country" (Joyce & Showers, 1988, p. 42). It is based on an expansive body of research on teacher expectations (see Rosenthal & Jacobson, 1968).

The principle underlying TESA is that teachers should ensure that their behaviors are equal and equitable for all students, thus creating an atmosphere in which all students feel accepted. In keeping with this principle, the program focuses on 15 teacher behaviors that are most often employed with perceived high achievers.

The behaviors are organized into three strands: response opportunities, feedback, and personal regard. The *response opportunities* strand addresses equitable distribution of positive types of responses, helping individual students, response latency (i.e., how long a teacher waits for a student's response), and types of questions. The *feedback* strand addresses affirmation of correct performance, praise and reasons for praise, listening, and accepting feelings. The *personal regard* strand addresses proximity, courtesy, personal interest, touching, and desisting. Although the initial research on TESA demonstrated that it positively affects teacher behavior, student behavior, and student achievement (see Kerman, Kimball, & Martin, 1980; Sadker & Sadker, 1994; Grayson & Martin, 1985), some research has shown mixed results for its effectiveness (see Gottfredson, Marciniak, Birdseye, & Gottfredson, 1995).

ActionSteps

ACTION STEP 1 ▼

Use specific techniques to establish an appropriate level of dominance in the classroom.

The core of effective teacher-student relationships is a healthy balance between dominance and cooperation. One thing that makes such a balance difficult is that students rely primarily on teacher behavior as the indication of whether the teacher is providing guidance or not and whether the teacher is cooperative or not. As Wubbels, Brekelmans, van Tartwijk, and Admiral (1999) explain:

> We consider every behavior that someone displays in the presence of someone else as a communication, and therefore we assume that in the presence of someone else one cannot *not* [original emphasis] communicate . . . Whatever someone's intentions are, the other persons in the communication will infer meaning from that someone's behavior. If, for example, teachers ignore students' questions, perhaps because they do not hear them, then students may not only get this inattention but also infer that the teacher is too busy or thinks that the students are too dull to understand or that the questions are impertinent. The message that students take from the teacher's negation can be different from the teacher's intention . . . (p. 153–154)

Operationally, this implies that you must balance those behaviors that communicate a proper level of dominance with those behaviors that communicate a proper level of cooperation. Here we first consider dominance behaviors. I should note that addressing rules and procedures and disciplinary interventions as described in Chapters 2 and 3 goes a long way toward communicating a proper level of dominance. That is, if you have established and implemented rules and procedures as well as positive and negative consequences, you will have certainly communicated your dominance. At least two other areas are important to this communication: exhibiting assertive behavior and establishing clear learning goals.

▶ Exhibiting Assertive Behavior

One of the best ways to communicate a proper level of dominance is to exhibit *assertive behavior*. According to Emmer, Evertson, and Worsham (2003), assertive behavior is "the ability to stand up for one's legitimate rights in ways that make it less likely that others will ignore or circumvent them" (p. 146). It is significantly different from both passive behavior and aggressive behavior. Emmer, Evertson, and Worsham describe assertive behavior that is tailored specifically to the classroom. They refer to their approach as "constructive assertiveness." They explain that "the adjective *constructive* implies that the teacher does not tear down or attack the student" (p. 146). It can be thought of as a set of relatively specific teacher behaviors that involve three primary categories:

1. Use of assertive body language: Making and keeping eye contact; maintaining an erect posture, facing the offending student but

keeping enough distance so as not to appear threatening; matching one's facial expression with the content of the message being presented to students.

2. Use of appropriate tone of voice: Speaking clearly and deliberately; using a pitch that is slightly but not greatly elevated from normal classroom speech; avoiding any indication of emotion in one's voice.

3. Persisting until the appropriate behavior is displayed: Not ignoring an inappropriate behavior; not being diverted by a student denying, arguing, or blaming; but listening to legitimate explanations.

The following vignettes depict teachers using assertive behavior at the elementary and secondary levels.

Elementary

Mr. Saunders always involves his 4th graders in the establishment of classroom rules and procedures. During class meetings, students can raise issues about the rules and even about the consequences and rewards related to those rules. But Mr. Saunders is also very clear that some issues are not up for discussion. "This is one Mr. Saunders gets to decide on his own," he states, when appropriate. Very early in the year, the students know there is no point in arguing when he has made this declaration.

Secondary

When a freshman in high school is angry, he can be intimidating. Ms. Palmer, a veteran teacher and a petite woman, has learned how to stand her ground with the angriest of students. When a student confronts her and begins to yell about a rule or a grade, Ms. Palmer stands straight, looks the student in the eye, and says, "I will be happy to talk to you when you're
speaking as calmly as I am." This rarely works the first time, but she repeats those exact words over and over, both as a way of communicating the message that she is willing to talk—on her terms—and as a way of reminding herself not to raise her own voice. Her calm, steadfast demeanor has the desired effect.

▶ Establishing Clear Learning Goals

A second way to exhibit proper levels of dominance is to be very clear about the learning goals that are to be addressed in a unit, a quarter, or a semester. Related behaviors include the following:

- Establishing learning goals at the beginning of a unit of instruction
- Providing feedback on those goals
- Continually and systematically revisiting the goals
- Providing summative feedback regarding the goals

To these ends, rubrics are an excellent tool. For example, assume that you have identified "understanding and utilizing fractions" as one of your learning goals for a unit. You might present students with the following rubric as a guide to your expectations regarding this topic:

4. You understand the characteristics of fractions along with the different types. You can accurately describe how fractions are related to decimals and percentages. You can convert fractions to decimals and can explain the process.

3. You understand the basic characteristics of fractions. You know how fractions are related to decimals and percentages. You can convert fractions to decimals.

2. You have a basic understanding of the following, but have some small misunderstandings with one or more: the characteristics of fractions; the relationship between fractions, decimals, and percentages; how to convert fractions to decimals.

1. You have some major problems or misunderstandings with one or more of the following: the characteristics of fractions; the relationship between fractions, decimals, and percentages; how to convert fractions to decimals.

The clarity of purpose provided by a rubric like this one goes a long way in communicating an appropriate level of dominance to students. Recall that dominance means that the teacher provides strong leadership not only in terms of classroom behavior but also in terms of the content addressed in the class. A detailed rubric says to students that you are clear about the content that will be addressed and the relative levels of importance of that content. It also communicates that you wish to lead the class by making the criteria for success highly visible. When you provide rubrics at the outset of a unit of instruction, you give students clear academic targets. Rubrics for specific types of content can be found in Marzano (2000b) and Marzano, Pickering, and McTighe (1993). The following vignettes depict how elementary and secondary teachers might effectively establish clear goals via the use of rubrics.

Elementary

"I get tired of kids asking what grade I am going to 'give' them. They earn the grades; I don't give the grade." Sam Flanders listened to the new teacher he was mentoring and then replied, "Let me tell you what I discovered about my own teaching when I

heard the same things from students. On reflection, I realized that when I graded papers, I assigned points for so many different reasons that it was no wonder students thought I gave grades. My assignments now are always accompanied by a list of learning goals and a rubric to accompany each goal. Students now know that to earn an A, for example, they have to show in-depth understanding of key ideas or a high level of competence in applying a key process. They no longer beg me to give them points; they know how to earn the grade."

Secondary

During writing conferences, Mrs. Blighten began to hear more and more resistance from students when she made suggestions for improving their work. They whined and moaned, "C'mon, you know what I meant," or "I think my work is fine the way it is." She finally concluded that her students thought they should be trying to please her instead of trying to improve their writing. "Probably," she thought to herself, "they don't take ownership of the writing goals because they don't understand the goals described in the district writing rubric." To remedy this, one day she distributed the district rubric for writing and worked with the students to generate a class rubric with "kid-friendly" language. The learning goals represented in the district rubric remained, but words familiar to the students, such as "awesome" and "wow," replaced the technical language. From then on, students used this rubric to self-assess their own writing—before the writing conferences—to identify their areas of strength and weakness. Once she started to use the rubric with students, Ms. Blighten noticed that students seemed to understand the writing goals, and conferences were focused more on student learning than on the grades.

ACTION STEP 2 ▼

Use specific behaviors that communicate an appropriate level of cooperation.

At least four specific types of behavior communicate an appropriate level of cooperation: providing flexible learning goals, taking a personal interest in students, using equitable and positive learning behaviors, and responding appropriately to students' incorrect responses.

▶ Providing Flexible Learning Goals

The preceding discussion explained how establishing clear learning goals communicates an appropriate level of dominance. However, some behaviors regarding learning goals also convey appropriate levels of cooperation. For example, allowing students to set some of their own learning goals at the beginning of a unit or asking students what they would like to learn conveys a sense of cooperation. To illustrate, assume that you have identified the topic of fractions as the focus of a unit of instruction and provided a rubric like that described above. In addition, though, you might ask students to identify some aspect of fractions or a related topic that is particularly interesting to them. This not only has the potential to increase students' interest in the topic, but also conveys the message that you are concerned about their interests and are making an attempt to include those interests in your instruction. The following vignettes exemplify how an elementary and a secondary teacher might establish flexible learning goals.

Elementary

The 3rd graders in Ms. Phillips's class were accustomed to using the KWL chart before specific lessons, but this time Ms. Phillips used it at the beginning of the entire unit on electricity. Before giving them the learning goals for the unit, she asked students what they already KNEW (K) about electricity, then asked what they WANTED (W) to learn. She recorded the students' ideas on the class chart. Ms. Phillips then handed out a list of the learning goals that were identified in the district curriculum guide for the electricity unit. "We need to achieve these district learning goals," explained Ms. Phillips, "but I want each of you to add some goals that interest you. Use our class KWL chart to stimulate your thinking." As they worked through the unit, Ms. Phillips noticed that some of the students' goals even got her more excited than the goals from the curriculum guide.

Secondary

Mr. Bard loved teaching Shakespeare and sometimes regretted that his students did not always share his excitement. Then one year he added the following learning goal to the unit: Students will understand and apply the characteristics of a "classic" in literature. *During the unit, students were required to study characteristics of a classic and to apply these characteristics to Shakespeare's plays to determine if, in fact, these plays could be considered classics. In addition, Mr. Bard asked students to identify another area where the word "classic" was used—areas such as movies, sports, fashion, cars, television, and music. He then asked students to select one area of interest to them, study the characteristics of a classic in that area, and apply these characteristics to identify true classics in their area of interest. The students, and Mr. Bard, had a wonderful time discovering how frequently the concept of classic could be applied to topics of interest to the students. Mr. Bard concluded that, with this additional learning goal, students showed more respect for his passion for Shakespeare because he demonstrated respect for their passions in the design of the unit.*

▶ Taking a Personal Interest in Students

It is probably little or no exaggeration to say that all students appreciate the personal attention of the teacher. In fact, for some students the need for the teacher to show some personal interest in them is paramount to their learning (McCombs & Whisler, 1997; Combs, 1982). Therefore, virtually anything you do to show interest in students as individuals has a positive impact on their learning. Here are some behaviors that communicate personal interest:

- Talking informally with students before, during, and after class about their interests
- Greeting students outside of school— for instance, at extracurricular events or at stores
- Singling out a few students each day in the lunchroom and talking to them
- Being aware of and commenting on important events in students' lives, such as participation in sports, drama, or other extracurricular activities
- Complimenting students on important achievements in and outside of school
- Meeting students at the door as they come into class and saying hello to each child, making sure to use his or her first name

The following vignettes show how an elementary and a secondary teacher might implement these behaviors.

Elementary

"I notice that whenever you doodle, it always has something to do with horses. I loved horses when I was a girl, too. Bring in some of your pictures, because I would love to see them; and they might help you with topics in your writing." Devon blushed with pleasure and surprise that her teacher actually noticed how passionate she was about horses. She never talked to anyone about her love of horses and didn't even realize her doodles were always horse-related until her teacher made the comment. She couldn't wait to bring in her horse pictures to show her teacher. She also noticed that she was actually excited about her next writing assignment—a story about a horse.

Secondary

When each issue of the school newspaper was released, Ms. Jackson read through every article. This was just one of the many techniques she used for discovering something about the interests of her students, especially those who were so quiet they almost became invisible. More than once she stared into stunned eyes when she asked students about their times in the track meet, their attendance at a debate, or their volunteer work at the animal clinic.

▶ Using Equitable and Positive Classroom Behaviors

Earlier in this chapter, we considered TESA as one program that is especially effective at fostering effective teacher-student relationships (Kerman, Kimball, & Martin, 1980; Sadker & Sadker, 1994; Grayson & Martin, 1985). The aspect of TESA that is particularly useful in terms of fostering teacher-student relationships is strategies for equitable and positive interactions. Such behaviors include the following:

- Making eye contact with each student in the room (which you can do by scanning the entire room as you speak); freely moving about all sections of the room.

• Over the course of a class period, deliberately moving toward and being close to each student; making sure that the seating arrangement allows you and the students clear and easy access to move around the room.

• Attributing the ownership of ideas to the students who initiated them. (For instance, in a discussion you might say, "Dennis has just added to Mary's idea by saying that . . . .")

• Allowing and encouraging all students to be part of class discussions and interactions; making sure to call on students who do not commonly participate, not just students who respond most frequently.

• Providing appropriate "wait time" for all students, regardless of their past performance or your perception of their abilities.

The following vignette depicts how one teacher used some of these techniques in the classroom.

When Ms. McIntyre facilitated a classroom discussion, she tried to let students do most of the talking, especially on the first day of a new topic. As she listened, she almost always typed students' questions and comments into presentation slides on her laptop computer, making sure she put students' names next to their comments. The next day, as the discussion began again, she projected her slides on the screen as a way of stimulating more in-depth discussion of some of the students' ideas from the day before. Even students who were reluctant to participate on the first day, or who were just too shy to chime in, knew that they could express their ideas privately to Ms. McIntyre and she would include their ideas in her slides. In this way, all students— those who were comfortable in class discussions and those who were reluctant—were encouraged to think through their ideas and to be ready to expand on those ideas.

▶ **Responding Appropriately to Students' Incorrect Responses**

Questioning is a common instructional activity in many classrooms. The manner in which you respond to a student's incorrect response or lack of response conveys a strong message to students (Hunter, 1969). When students respond incorrectly or make no response at all to a question you have posed, they are particularly vulnerable. Your behavior at these critical junctures goes a long way toward establishing a relationship that enhances or detracts from student learning. Useful behaviors in these situations include the following:

• Emphasizing what was right. Giving credit to the aspects of an incorrect response that are correct and acknowledging when the student is headed in the right direction. Identifying the question that the incorrect response answered.

• Encouraging collaboration. Allowing students time to seek help from peers. This can result in better responses and can enhance learning.

• Restating the question. Asking the question a second time and allowing time for students to think before you expect a response.

• Rephrasing the question. Paraphrasing the question or asking it from a different perspective, one that may give students a better understanding of the question.

• Giving hints or cues. Providing enough guidance so that students gradually come up with the answer.

• Providing the answer and asking for elaboration. If a student absolutely cannot come up with the correct answer, providing it for him and then asking him to say it in his own words or providing another example of the answer.

• Respecting the student's option to pass, when appropriate.

The following vignette illustrates some of these behaviors.

> *David's worst nightmare was to be called on in class and feel every eye on him as the teacher waited for an answer. Even when he knew the answer, he always became so self-conscious that his mind became a blank. It was even worse when the teacher, although well intentioned, responded to his silence with overly kind comments such as, "That's OK, David. Don't worry." However, things were different in Mr. Prost's class. It is easy to understand why David, and many other students, loved his approach to class discussions. Mr. Prost would often write on the white board the major questions that he planned to ask during class. He would then start by saying, "Look at the first question. Turn to your partner and give him or her your best answer to the question. You have three minutes. Go." After the three minutes, Mr. Prost would call on students for the answer. Students had the option of providing their own answers, quoting their partners' answers, or asking their partners to quote them. If the answer was incorrect, no one student felt singled out. When students gave several incorrect answers, Mr. Prost allowed another three minutes for collaboration. For David, this approach worked perfectly. His anxieties about being wrong, and being alone, were so relieved that he began to shine in that class, revealing his true depth of knowledge.*

Action Step 3 ▼

Be aware of the needs of different types of students.

As discussed earlier, effective classroom managers are aware of the unique needs of indi-

vidual students, particularly those from backgrounds that include experiences like those presented in Figure 4.4. Although many teachers sense such needs instinctively, it is useful to formally identify categories of high-need students and the management strategies that are most effective within each category. Categories of high-need students have been identified by Jere Brophy (1996) and by Brenda Freeman (1994). Building on the works of Brophy and Freeman, Figure 4.5 shows five categories of high-need students: (1) passive, (2) aggressive, (3) attention problems, (4) perfectionist, and (5) socially inept. The first three categories have been divided into subcategories to provide a more detailed description of the variations in student behavior that you might encounter.

▶ Passive

The category of *passive* is divided into two subcategories, *fear of relationships* and *fear of failure*. Although fear is the common denominator in both subcategories, the object of the fear is different. Some students in the passive category may be victims of neglect and abuse that is physical or verbal in nature. They may also suffer from medical problems including but not limited to depression and social phobias. These students will exhibit fear of relationships. Other students in the passive category may suffer from a deeply engrained belief that they do not have the requisite skills to succeed in school. These students will exhibit fear of failure. As with all the other categories in Figure 4.5, it is important to remember that the behaviors of these students are deeply rooted in causal factors that originate outside the classroom. Therefore, it is unreasonable to expect these students to be able to change their behaviors easily.

Figure 4.5
Five Categories of High-Need Students

Category	Subcategory
Passive	Fear of relationships
	Fear of failure
Aggressive	Hostile
	Oppositional
	Covert
Attention Problems	Hyperactive
	Inattentive
Perfectionist	None
Socially Inept	None

The following vignettes depict the type of interactions that are particularly effective with these types of students. You will note that all vignettes in this section depict one-to-one conversations between teacher and student. This is because interventions with the types of students described in this section typically require extraordinary personal attention from you, the teacher.

Passive: Fear of Relationships

Drake is a shy, reserved child. He will not ask questions in class and has difficulty answering when called on. He often looks down and seems sad. Other students tend to tease him or ignore him, as do many adults. His performance in class is probably average, but he seems capable of much more.

To reach Drake, Ms. Blake, his teacher, takes an approach that is not too direct. Rather, her strategy is to slowly develop a relationship with Drake and gain his trust. One of her first conversations with Drake proceeds as follows:

Ms. Blake: "Drake, I've noticed that you really tried hard on this last assignment."
Drake: [No response]
Ms. Blake: "I wanted you to know, I do notice you and your work even though you don't talk a lot."
Drake: "Thanks."
Ms. Blake: "If it's all right with you, I'll call on you a little more in class. I'd also like to talk to you privately every once in a while to see how you are doing."
Drake: "OK." With a slight smile, Drake walks away.

In the days and weeks following the conversation Ms. Blake follows through on her promise to call on Drake more frequently and to have a few private conversations. She takes particular care not to overwhelm Drake but slowly and gently increases the amount of contact and trust between them. The principle guiding her interactions with Drake is to exhibit kindness, consistency, and encouragement.

Passive: Fear of Failure

Beverly pouts a lot in class and seems to dislike school. She's been tested for learning disabilities and ADHD, and the results were negative. She rarely turns in her class work and produces sloppy work when she does. When questioned about this, she has no clear answers, just a lot of excuses that frequently begin with the words "I can't."

To establish a relationship, Mr. Waters has the following conversation with Beverly:

Mr. Waters: "Beverly, I would like to find out from you what is really causing your difficulties with your schoolwork."

Beverly: "I don't know." Beverly looks confused and on the spot.

Mr. Waters: "I know you are really bright, but somehow that's not showing up in your work. So, do you feel you could do better? I certainly do."

Beverly: "Probably not. I'm not very smart."

Mr. Waters: "Why do you say that? I really want to know."

Beverly: "I never do anything right. It doesn't matter anyway."

Mr. Waters: "It matters to me, Beverly. When was the last time you thought you did well at something? Not just school stuff?"

Beverly: "Never."

Mr. Waters: "Do you have hobbies or sports that you like?"

Beverly: "Well, I guess I do okay at piano and maybe reading my books at home."

Mr. Waters: "How did you get good at those things?"

Beverly: "Well, I guess I do them a lot and I don't get graded on them either. I like doing them."

Mr. Waters: "What else? Do you concentrate more?"

Beverly: "I pay more attention, and I don't rush so much."

Mr. Waters: "How would it be if you did that at school with your work, and I'll help you out, too?"

Beverly: "I'd probably do better."

Mr. Waters: "Let's give it a try, okay?"

Mr. Waters continues to have casual discussions with Beverly, always trying to emphasize the point that she is very successful at some things. He also meets with Beverly before and after significant classroom assignments. Before these assignments, they plan about what Beverly can do to keep herself on task and not give up. After the assignments, they both evaluate what worked and what did not work about their strategy.

▶ **Aggressive**

The category of *aggressive* students comprises three subcategories: *hostile, oppositional,* and *covert.* These categories closely correspond to diagnoses in the *Diagnostic and Statistical Manual* (DSM), published by the American Psychiatric Association (American Psychiatric Association, 2000). Although as a classroom teacher you cannot make formal diagnoses, it is useful to be conversant with the DSM and the descriptions of the various types of behaviors it contains. It is available in most bookstores.

The subcategory *hostile* is closely related to the clinical diagnosis of *conduct disorder* in the DSM. Characteristics of this disorder are poor anger control, poor impulse control, low capacity for empathy, a heightened sense of entitlement (i.e., "the world owes me"), inability to see the consequences of one's actions, low self-esteem (though students may not be able to admit it to themselves), propensity for thrill-seeking behavior, and a propensity to align with deviant peer groups and criminal behavior. Hostile students tend to give teachers and schools the most difficulty, take up much classroom time, and require schools and districts to provide added resources in terms of time, energy, and actual dollars to address the problems they create. For these reasons, they are the most widely researched group of problem students. It is important to remember that although they appear to be highly resistant to behavior change, hostile students are simply children experiencing a massive amount of fear and pain.

The second subcategory of aggressive students is referred to as *oppositional*. These students exhibit milder forms of behavior problems than do hostile students. This subcategory closely relates to the *oppositional-defiant* classification in the DSM. Typical characteristics of these students include consistent resistance to following rules, arguing with adults, frequent use of harsh, angry language, and a propensity to criticize, blame, and annoy others.

The subcategory of *covert* students does not have an identifiable DSM diagnosis, but these students are easily recognizable to most

teachers. They may be quite pleasant and even charming at times. However, they are often around or nearby when trouble starts, and they never quite do what is asked of them even though they convey a pleasant demeanor. They seem to operate at the periphery of disruptive behavior, engaging in activities that skirt the letter of the law. Consequently, they avoid punishment and the necessary attention to their behavior.

The following vignettes depict interactions with these three types of students.

Aggressive-Hostile

Michelle is out of control at home and at school. She is verbally abusive to anyone who gets in her way. She throws school supplies around, slams her locker shut, and may be responsible for school vandalism. She is in and out of the vice principal's office often but never seems to improve her behavior.

Michelle requires a schoolwide solution, and possibly referrals to outside interventions, such as individual therapy and group programs. The beginning point for a successful intervention is a meeting involving Michelle, school officials, and her parents. In that meeting a program is established that focuses on providing specific rewards for positive behavior and specific consequences for negative behavior. Michelle is an active participant in that meeting, particularly in terms of identifying those things she considers to be rewards or positive consequences. The initial meeting with Michelle proceeds as follows:

Teacher: "Michelle, what are some activities you'd like to do at home or school, things that you've always wanted to do?"

Michelle: "I'd like to switch from math to photography."

Teacher: "What else?"

Michelle: "I want to get my parents off my back."

Teacher: "Good. We're going to try to see that you get more of these things you like. But you are going to be the one to determine if you get them or not."

To clarify the expectations and specifics of the program that is being established for Michelle, everyone at the meeting contributes ideas that are incorporated into a chart (see Figure 4.6). The meeting continues until everyone—particularly Michelle—agrees that the program is workable. Michelle's parents agree that they will stop "getting on Michelle's back" and let the program play itself out. Each month the teacher, Michelle's parents, and Michelle meet to review her progress and to make changes in the program as needed.

Aggressive-Oppositional

Jake is a source of frustration for his teacher, Ms. McNulty, and his classmates alike. It seems he always tries to do the opposite of what is asked of him, regardless of how much trouble he gets into. He seems to like getting attention but for all the wrong things. Ms. McNulty finally has a meeting with Jake.

Figure 4.6

A Sample Chart for Behavior Management of an Aggressive/Hostile Student

Type of Behavior	Michelle's Behavior	Rewards and Consequences
Excellent Behavior	Polite and helpful with teachers and other students Grades: *B*s and *C*s	Acknowledgment by class Allowed two free-choice activities to do at home or school
Good Behavior	Pleasant enough Minimal disruptive behavior Grades: *C*s and *D*s	Allowed one free-choice activity to do at home or school Stays after school to finish homework
Poor Behavior	Angry, destructive behavior toward others and/or property Grades: *D*s or *F*s Truancy, tardiness	Detention, community service, extra work after school
Unacceptable Behavior	Violent to others or property	Suspended Put in treatment program

Ms. McNulty: "Jake, I've noticed that in general you are a great kid and really fun to be around. Sometimes, however, you seem to do the opposite of what I ask. For example, when I asked you to sit quietly at your seat today, you continued to laugh and get out of your seat. Have you noticed this pattern too?"

Jake: "Whatever."

Ms. McNulty: "I've told you before that your behavior is disruptive to the class, and your grades are falling because of it. With your help, I'd like to put a program in place to make things better for you and for me and for the whole class. Will you help me figure this out?"

Jake: "Like what?"

Ms. McNulty: "What is the best part of the day for you?"

Jake: "Being at recess."

Ms. McNulty: "What's the worst part of school for you?"

Jake: "Detention."

With this information, Ms. McNulty and Jake create a chart that details specific types of behavior with related positive and negative consequences (see Figure 4.7).

Ms. McNulty assures Jake that her intentions are not to punish him. Rather she wants to help him learn how to control his behavior so that he can enjoy class and get the grades he wants and deserves. Periodically, Ms. McNulty and Jake meet to reevaluate the behavioral chart they have created.

Aggressive-Covert

Amy always seems to be nearby when trouble occurs. She doesn't do anything

---

Figure 4.7

A Sample Chart for Behavior Management of an Aggressive/Oppositional Student

Type of Behavior	Jake's Behavior	Rewards and Consequences
Excellent Behavior	Follows instructions almost all the time Stays in seat Doesn't create trouble	Recess every day
Good Behavior	Follows instructions most of the time Stays in seat most of the time Creates trouble sometimes	Recess 3 times a week Detention once a week
Poor Behavior	Doesn't follow instructions Gets out of seat Creates trouble	No recess Detention 3 times a week

extremely negative or overt, but teases, pulls pranks, and gossips about others until they get mad. It takes a while for Mr. Hardwick, the teacher, to realize that Amy has a behavioral problem. When he does, he starts making notes about Amy's inappropriate behavior. Finally he takes Amy aside and has the following conversation:

Mr. Hardwick: "Amy, I hope you know that I like you and that many times I really enjoy your participation in class. However, it seems to me that you tend to do things that get other people in trouble. Do you know what I'm talking about?

Amy: "No."

Mr. Hardwick: "Let me tell you what I see. I notice that sometimes you talk to people and then they get in a fight, or you'll take people's things and hide them and then chuckle when they get upset — I've seen you! Pretty creative. But it does cause problems for others, right?"

Amy: "I guess so."

Mr. Hardwick: "We're going to have to do something about this. I'd like to solve this problem with your help."

Amy: "But it's not my fault!"

Mr. Hardwick: "Not totally. Others are responsible for their behavior too. But I don't think you're innocent either. Do you?"

Amy: "I guess not."

The conversation continues until Amy finally sees that Mr. Hardwick is serious and has a good grasp of what has been going on. Together they identify specific behaviors Amy will try to avoid. They also identify some things Amy considers to be a reward for the effort she will make as well as some negative consequences if she continues to exhibit the identified inappropriate behaviors. Periodically Mr. Hardwick and Amy meet to discuss how the plan is working.

▶ **Attention Problems**

The category of *attention problems* contains two subcategories: *hyperactive* and *inattentive*. Both closely correspond to specific DSM diagnoses. The subcategory of hyperactive corresponds to the DSM diagnoses of *attention deficit/hyperactive disorder, predominately hyperactive-impulsive type*. The subcategory of inattentive corresponds to the DSM classification of *attention deficit/hyperactivity disorder, predominately inattentive type*. Characteristics of the hyperactive subcategory include poor impulse control, inability to stay seated or work quietly, propensity to blurt out questions and answers, trouble taking turns, and propensity to interrupt others. Characteristics of the inattentive subcategory include failing to give close attention to details, rarely appearing to listen, having difficulty organizing tasks, forgetfulness in daily activities, and being easily distracted by extraneous stimuli. Students with this type of problem tend to be more anxious, whereas hyperactive students tend to be more impulsive (Erk, 2000). The following vignettes exemplify how you might interact with students with these two types of attention problems.

Attention Problems–Hyperactive

In class, David never seems to stop talking, moving, fidgeting, and telling jokes. He distracts others and rarely turns in his homework. He's bright, but his grades are well below his capabilities. He is quite likable at times, but generally wastes a lot of class time with his antics. His parents refuse to help him with medication or therapy, leaving the teacher, Ms. Paynter, with little outside help. After a number of attempts to gain David's attention, Ms. Paynter has the following conversation with him:

Ms. Paynter: "David, you seem to have real trouble sitting still. Would you agree with that?"

David: "I hate school and it's boring."

Ms. Paynter: "I know you sometimes have trouble concentrating. I'd like to suggest some things that will help you focus better. I'd like to spend some time helping you organize your assignments and write out how to do each project step by step so that in the future you can follow these steps. Let's also put you in a different place in the room so you have less to distract you."

The first thing Ms. Paynter does is to move David to a place in the class where it is easy for her to attend to David and for David to be more involved in what she is doing. For each major assignment, Ms. Paynter takes time to help David organize and prioritize what he will do to complete the assignment. Ms. Paynter and David keep meeting to discuss his progress.

Attention Problems–Inattentive

Cathy is a quiet adolescent who gets very frustrated when she can't do her school-work. She believes she is stupid and is becoming apathetic. After repeated failures, she has developed the habit of procrastinating. When she realizes her assignments are going to be late, she gets upset and turns in half-completed projects. She is thinking about dropping out of school and getting a job. Her parents are opposed to medication and therapy. When things look like they couldn't get much worse, Mr. Muuger sets up a meeting with Cathy.

Mr. Muuger: "Cathy, it seems to me that you are very frustrated and upset with school and with yourself. What's going on with you?"

Cathy: "I've tried for all these years and I can't stand it anymore. I am so ridiculously stupid!"

Mr. Muuger: "I wish someone would have helped you sooner. Has anyone ever given you tips about how to do better in school?"

Cathy: "Not really. Mostly I was told to try harder, but I don't know what that means. I try hard now."

Mr. Muuger provides Cathy with some concrete suggestions about how to study. He buys a book for Cathy on study skills. They meet periodically and go over some of the suggestions in the book together. They even brainstorm some ideas about things Cathy can do when she gets confused or gets "lost in the fog," as Cathy would say.

▶ Perfectionist

The category of *perfectionist* closely corresponds to the DSM diagnosis of *obsessive-compulsive personality disorder*. Perfectionist students are driven to succeed at levels that are close to, if not, unattainable. These students are often self-critical, have low self-esteem, and have deep-seated feelings of inferiority and vulnerability. They see being perfect as the only way to gain love, respect, or attention. At some level, they believe that they are liked or loved for what they can produce, not who they are. When confronted with a situation in which they feel they can't produce exceptional results, they may give up altogether, procrastinate, or make up excuses why they can't perform the task. As perfectionist children develop into adulthood, many of their behaviors are greatly rewarded because of their high output, minimal complaining, and willingness to put in long hours often for little or no financial reward. However, the end result of perfectionism can be self-destructive behaviors and thinking patterns that eventually lead to depression and even suicide (Blatt, 1995). The following vignette depicts how a teacher might interact with a perfectionist student.

Matt tries to be perfect at everything he does. Good isn't good enough. His desk is never left with anything out of place; his homework is in on time and complete with all directions followed to the letter. Yet Matt doesn't enjoy his success. He is constantly berating himself under his breath if he doesn't do as well as he expects. When things don't go well in his eyes, he has a hard time recomposing himself. Matt also has a tendency to be harsh and critical of others. His classmates are jealous of his success on one hand but also dislike his negativity. He won't try new things if he isn't sure he can succeed. When an opportunity arises, Ms. Becker, the teacher, has a private conversation with Matt.

Ms. Becker: "Matt, let's talk. You are really trying hard for all A's and to be the best runner on the track team, and I admire that a lot. Sometimes, though, you seem awfully hard on yourself and say mean things to yourself. I've noticed that sometimes the standards you hold for yourself are unrealistic. I couldn't do much of what you expect of yourself. It also seems to me that you put high expectations on others. When they don't succeed, you criticize them like you criticize yourself. It all seems a bit harsh."

Matt: "Well, shouldn't I try to be the best?"

Ms. Becker: "Some of what you do will get you far in life, like your desire to learn and compete. However, other things you do will make life harder for you in the long run. For instance, when you criticize yourself so strongly, you take away your ability or willingness to try again. When you criticize others, they end up disliking you. What about doing it this way: when you or others make a mistake, just acknowledge that it was a mistake and that you, like everybody else, sometimes have to make mistakes to learn."

Matt: "Hadn't thought of that."

Ms. Becker: "How about helping those kids who are struggling with their schoolwork? You might find that it is one of the best ways to make friends—by giving people a hand. Here's another idea. Try being very positive about your mistakes one day, then very harsh and critical the next day. Switch back and forth for a while and see which one you like better and which produces better results for you."

Periodically, Ms. Becker calls Matt aside for similar conversations. Over time Matt starts to see the negative consequences of his perfectionism and develops techniques to counteract them.

▶ Socially Inept

Socially inept children have difficulty making and keeping friends. They stand too close and touch others in annoying ways, talk too much, make "stupid" or embarrassing remarks, misread others' comments, and, in general, don't seem to fit in. They are often well-meaning students who are trying too hard to relate to others and are baffled by the animosity others show them. These children often feel sad, confused, and different from others, and they have difficulty following complex sequences of events. Their behavior is often labeled as immaturity, tactlessness, and insensitivity. Parents often report that these children seemed different from birth (Nowicki & Duke, 1992). The following vignette depicts how a teacher might interact with a socially inept student.

Jason consistently has trouble making and keeping friends at school, and his mother says he has almost no friends at home either. His loud, "over the top," annoying behavior irritates others. He talks too much, doesn't listen, and stands too close to people. In general, he tries too hard to make friends and ends up getting teased and isolated. It affects his schoolwork because he is frequently upset. One day, Mr. Ciccinelli, his teacher, happens to overhear Jason say, "I don't understand why nobody likes me. I'm nice to people." Mr. Ciccinelli calls Jason aside, and they have the following conversation.

Mr. Ciccinelli: "Jason, I heard you say that nobody likes you. I've noticed that you are having a hard time making friends in class. Would you like me to make some suggestions? I'd like to help."

Jason: "Sure, anything."

Mr. Ciccinelli: "Let's experiment. What if I stand too close to you and speak loudly like this, how do you feel?"

Jason: "Like I want to back away."

Mr. Ciccinelli: "Well, sometimes I see you do that with some of the other students in class. Did you know that?"

Jason: "Not really."

Mr. Ciccinelli: "How about if you stand further away and talk in a softer voice? That way it's easier for people to be with you."

Jason: "I could do that."

Mr. Ciccinelli: "Let me ask you another question. Do you like people who want you to talk or people who talk a lot about themselves?"

Jason: "People who listen to me."

Mr. Ciccinelli: "When you are talking to others, are you focused on what they are saying or are you thinking of what you will say next?"

Jason: "I'm not so sure."

Mr. Ciccinelli: "Try listening a lot, even if you think you can't stand it anymore, and see if you understand what they are trying to say before you talk. It's worth a try. Maybe you will find out that you get along better with people that way."

Mr. Ciccinelli keeps meeting with Jason, informally discussing how things are going and coming up with new ideas that Jason then tries out.

Summary

Teacher-student relationships are critical to the success of two of the other aspects of effective classroom management—rules and procedures, and disciplinary interventions. To build good relationships with students, it is important to communicate appropriate levels of dominance and to let students know that you are in control of the class and are willing and able to lead. It's also important to communicate appropriate levels of cooperation and to convey the message that you are interested in the concerns of students as individuals and the class as a whole. You may need to make a special effort to build positive relationships with high-need students, but using the proper techniques in working with these students can enhance the chance of successful classroom management.

5

MENTAL SET

The final factor important to effective classroom management is an appropriate mental set. Of the four elements outlined in Chapter 1, this is probably the most unusual, at least in terms of its title—mental set. But looking at Figure 1.3 in Chapter 1, we see that my meta-analysis shows that this element has the largest effect size. Specifically, the average effect size for mental set is –1.294 as compared to –.909 for disciplinary interventions, –.869 for teacher-student relationships, and –.763 for rules and procedures. Although the label "mental set" might be unusual in the parlance of education, it is highly descriptive of a critical aspect of effective classroom management. Effective managers approach the classroom with a specific frame of mind—a specific mental set.

The Research and Theory

The construct of a mental set in classroom management is quite similar to the construct of "mindfulness" in psychology. Mindfulness was popularized by Ellen Langer in a series of works (Langer, 1989; Langer & Rodin, 1976; Langer & Weinman, 1981). Langer explains that mindfulness involves a heightened sense of situational awareness and a conscious control over one's thoughts and behavior relative to that situation. This frame of mind is not easy to cultivate and maintain because the human brain is predisposed to focus on a very narrow range of stimuli and to operate quite automatically relative to those stimuli. That is, we typically do not attend to all of what is happening around us. In fact, we commonly operate with very little conscious awareness of our environment, particularly regarding routine activities. An interesting, albeit contrived, way to observe this phenomenon is to read the sentence below once and only once. While doing so, count the number of times the letter *F* appears. Remember, read the sentence once only:

FINAL FOLIOS SEEM TO RESULT FROM YEARS OF DUTIFUL STUDY OF TEXTS ALONG WITH YEARS OF SCIENTIFIC EXPERIENCE

How many times does the letter *F* appear? The answer is eight times. If you perform as most people do on this task, you did not discern all eight *F*s. This is because we do not process words on a letter-by-letter or even a word-by-word basis when we read. Rather, we use very little visual information to recognize words as quickly as possible. Additionally, we spend very little energy on the function words such as *of* and *from* because we can infer that they are there from our knowledge of English syntax. Given that you paid little attention to the function words, you might have missed the three *F*s that appear in the three *of*s and the *F* in *from*. Although this is a contrived example, it illustrates the fact that our typical frame of mind is not one that is disposed to noticing detail or deviations from our expectations.

For the most part, this poses no problem in our lives, yet this mode of operating sometimes produces humorous encounters. Langer (1989) relates the following examples:

> Have you ever said "excuse me" to a store mannequin or written a check in January with the previous year's date? When in this mode, we take in and use limited signals from the world around us (the female form, the familiar face of the check) without letting signals (the motionless pose, a calendar) penetrate as well. . . .
>
> . . . Once, in a small department store, I gave a cashier a new credit card. Noticing that I hadn't signed it, she handed it back to me to sign. Then she took my credit card, passed it through

her machine, handed me the resulting form, and asked me to sign it. I did as I was told. The cashier then held the forms to the newly signed card to see if the signatures matched (pp. 12–13).

Langer refers to this automatic, unconscious way of interacting with the world as "mindlessness." This is the antithesis of the mental set teachers must have for effective classroom management. Specifically, the mental set necessary for effective classroom management requires teachers to cultivate a mindful stance relative to their "withitness" and "emotional objectivity." Both of these constructs have strong research support relative to their effectiveness. The results of my meta-analysis for these factors appear in Figure 5.1.

Figure 5.1 illustrates that within the category of mental set, withitness had the greater average effect size of –1.417, which translates into a change of 42 percentile points in the average amount of disruptive behavior. Again, I must caution that this extremely large effect size is based on relatively few studies (3) and relatively few subjects (426) and would probably be lower if more studies were available. With this caution noted, the average effect size of –1.417 provides evidence for the powerful impact of withitness. What is this behavior with the unusual name?

The term *withitness* was coined by Jacob Kounin, who is generally considered the first researcher to systematically study the characteristics of effective classroom managers. As described in Chapter 1, Kounin carried out his initial research by carefully examining videotapes of classroom teachers. He concluded that one of the primary differences between effective versus ineffective managers was not in how they handled the disruptive behavior

Figure 5.1

Effect Sizes for Mental Set

	Average Effect Size	95% Confidence Interval	Number of Subjects	Number of Studies	Percentile Decrease in Disruptions
Mental Set (General)	−1.294	(−1.098) to (−1.489)	502	5	40
Withitness	−1.417	(−1.202) to (−1.644)	426	3	42
Emotional Objectivity	−.705	(−.228) to (−1.181)	76	2	26

Note: Data were not available to compute average effect sizes for various grade level intervals.

of students, but in the disposition of the teacher to quickly and accurately identify problem behavior or potential problem behavior and to act on it immediately. He referred to this disposition as *withitness:*

> Classroom management is unrelated to how you handle misbehavior and how you handle misbehavior is unrelated to the amount of misbehavior you get. There is one exception. For example, two boys are in the back of the class during an arithmetic lesson. One of them grabs the other's paper and the second one grabs his paper. Then the first one pokes the second in the shoulder jokingly and the other one pokes the first, then they chase each other around the table laughing, then one pulls the shirt off the other and the second pulls his shirt off. Then he unzips the second's fly and he unzips the first guy's fly and the teacher says, "Boys, stop that!" We said that was too late. So it wasn't how she said "stop it" or whether she walked closer or didn't walk closer. Or whether she threatened or didn't threaten. It was whether she demonstrated to the class that she knew what was going on, that

she had eyes in the back of her head. It was not whether she came in right away but whether she came in before something spread or became more serious. And we gave that the technical term of withitness. That is the only thing that correlated with management success. (1983, p. 7)

Brophy describes withitness in more technical and less anecdotal terms. He explains:

> Remaining "with it" (aware of what is happening in all parts of the classroom at all times) by continuously scanning the classroom, even when working with small groups or individuals. Also demonstrating this withitness to students by intervening promptly and accurately when inappropriate behavior threatens to become disruptive. This minimizes timing errors (failing to notice and intervene until an incident has already become disruptive) and target errors (mistakes in identifying the students responsible for the problem). (1996, p. 11)

Finally, in their book *Looking in Classrooms*, Good and Brophy (2003) describe withitness as depicted in Kounin's work in the following way:

> . . . Effective managers monitored their classroom regularly. They positioned themselves so that they could see all students and they continuously scanned the room to keep track of what was going on, no matter what else they were doing at the time. They also let their students know that they were "with it"—aware of what was happening and likely to detect inappropriate behavior early and accurately. This enabled them to nip problems in the bud before they could escalate into serious disruptions. If they found it necessary to intervene directly to stop misbehavior, they focused on the students who started the problem or were most responsible for its escalation. If they were uncertain about who was most responsible for the problem, they simply told the entire group involved to resume working on their assignments (to avoid publicly blaming the wrong student). (p. 112)

Although it might appear that "withitness" does not translate into specific behavior, in fact, it is a learnable skill. Indeed, Evertson (1995) has shown that many aspects of withitness can be taught and reinforced in a relatively short period of time.

The second aspect of an appropriate mental set for classroom management is "emotional objectivity." Stated differently, an effective classroom manager implements and enforces rules and procedures, executes disciplinary actions, and (even) cultivates effective relationships with students without interpreting violations of classroom rules and procedures, negative reactions to disciplinary actions, or lack of response to the teacher's attempts to forge relationships as a personal attack. As Ron Nelson, Ron Martella, and Benita Galand (1998) note, emotional objectivity allows the teacher to address disciplinary issues in an "unemotional, matter-of-fact" manner (p. 156). Robert and Ruth Soar (1979) emphasize the importance of emotional objectivity, noting that when teachers are not emotionally objective, they run the risk of undermining their entire classroom management system.

The importance of emotional objectivity was also demonstrated by Jere Brophy and Carolyn Evertson (1976) in their study of the classroom practices of teachers who consistently produce achievement gains greater than expected as compared to a randomly selected group of teachers. They note:

> The successful teachers usually had quite realistic attitudes toward students and teacher-student relationships. Although they liked the children and enjoyed interpersonal aspects of teaching, they took a professional view of their students, looking upon them primarily as young learners with whom they interacted within a teacher-student relationship. In contrast, the less successful teachers tended to take one of two contradictory extreme overreactions to students. The more common of these was a romanticized notion of the student as a warm, wonderful, lovely, precious, etc. person who was a great pleasure just to be around. In our observations, teachers who painted this rosy picture of students were not more likely to be warm toward them or to appear to be enjoying more realistic views. In fact, a few of the more gushy teachers had highly chaotic classrooms . . . which occasionally became so out of control that the teacher exploded in anger and punitiveness in spite of herself . . .

There also were a few disillusioned and bitter teachers who looked upon students as "the enemy." (pp. 43–44)

Additionally, they note:

> We thought that the warmer, more affectionate teachers generally would be more effective than other teachers, particularly in low SES schools. As it turned out, teacher affectionateness did not show this relationship. It was unrelated, either linearly or curvilinearly, to students' learning gains. (p. 109)

Some teachers with whom I have discussed the disposition of emotional objectivity have reacted negatively, noting that it seems to take the "personal element" out of teacher-student interactions. If teachers are objective, then they, by definition, are keeping a distance from their students. Although it is true that keeping a certain psychological distance from students is necessary for effective classroom management, this does not have to translate into aloofness with students. It simply means carrying out the various aspects of classroom management without becoming emotionally involved regarding the outcomes—without personalizing the actions of students. This is very difficult to do because the normal human reaction to student disobedience or lack of response is to feel hurt or even angry. Such high-arousal emotional states do not provide a good basis on which to implement rules, execute disciplinary actions, or establish relationships.

Programs

Mental set as defined in this chapter is the classroom management factor that is usually not addressed directly in classroom manage-

ment programs. That is, one does not generally find classroom management programs that address the constructs of withitness or emotional objectivity by name. However, a number of programs address the component skills associated with these two constructs. For example, the Classroom Organization and Management Program, or COMP (Evertson, 1995), provides strategies for enhancing teachers' situational awareness of the potential problems in the classroom. Think Time (Nelson & Carr, 1999) addresses emotional objectivity in some depth, particularly in situations when a teacher is employing disciplinary procedures in the classroom and when students are in the Think Time classroom (see Chapter 3 and Chapter 8 for discussions). Finally, Assertive Discipline (Canter & Canter, 1992) addresses strategies for enhancing withitness as well as strategies for developing and maintaining a healthy emotional tone.

ActionSteps

ACTION STEP 1 ▼

Employ specific techniques to maintain or heighten your awareness of the actions of students in your classes (withitness).

The very term *withitness* might make it appear that this characteristic does not lend itself to development. You either are "withit" or you're not. In fact, you can take at least three concrete actions to enhance your "withitness": react immediately, forecast problems, and observe a master teacher.

▶ Reacting Immediately

Virtually all examples of withitness explicitly note that teachers who have mastered this disposition frequently scan the classroom, particularly when working with a small group of students or an individual student (see Berliner, 1986; Brophy, 1996; Kounin, 1983). Stated differently, one behavioral characteristic of withitness is to periodically and systematically scan the classroom, noting the behaviors of individual students or groups of students. If anything inappropriate is occurring, attention is turned to it immediately. If you believe that you are not highly aware of what your students are doing, you can practice the simple behavior of looking around the room for indications of potential or actual disruption on a frequent and periodic basis. Here is a specific technique to try when you are engaged in whole-class instruction:

- Walk around the classroom, making sure you spend some time in each quadrant.
- Periodically scan the faces of the students in the class, making eye contact with each student if possible.
- As you scan the classroom, pay particular attention to incidents or behaviors that look like they could turn into problems.
- Make eye contact with those students involved in the incident or who are exhibiting the behavior.
- If this doesn't work, move toward the students.
- If the behavior or incident continues, say something to the students, keeping the comments as private as possible.

When you are working with an individual student or a small group of students, you can use the same technique, but simply begin by periodically looking up from the individual or the group to make eye contact with the other students in the class.

The following vignette describes one teacher's withitness.

> *"It's cool. She doesn't yell or glare or anything. She just looks." McKinley, an 8th grader, was describing her math teacher, Ms. Clark, who is known for keeping her students on task and doing so without sending kids to the office or to detention. Whether working with small groups or talking to the entire class, Ms. Clark always notices when kids are beginning to talk or behave inappropriately. No matter what she is doing, she stops, and in an almost frozen position, she makes eye contact with the student or students. Her Mona Lisa–like expression shows no negative emotion, only rapt attention. If the offending students do not notice at first, their peers alert them. When they stop their disruptive behavior, which is almost always in seconds, she continues where she left off. The polite attention and silence both set a positive tone and get the desired results.*

▶ Forecasting Problems

Another technique that enhances your withitness is to mentally review what might go wrong with specific students in specific classes and the way you will address these potential problems. The categories of students described in Chapter 4—aggressive, passive, attention problems, perfectionist, and socially inept—are particularly useful for this purpose. If you have students who fall within these categories, you can think through potential issues that might arise with them before meeting with the class. For example, you might know that a perfectionist student in one of your classes frequently becomes agitated when she is having difficulty understanding something you are presenting or difficulty completing an assigned activity. If you know that difficult content or a difficult assignment is going to be part of an upcoming class, you can think through how you might interact with the student to head off potential problems. A hyperactive student (one of the subcategories of attention problems) in one of your classes might have difficulty attending to classroom activities immediately after lunch. Knowing that you will be working with him after lunch, you might identify those things you can do to head off potential problems or suggestions you can make to the student to avoid behavior problems. The following vignette depicts how this behavior might appear in the classroom.

Ms. Wilson knew that the first day of the new group project was going to be tough for some of her students. Further, she predicted that when the students became frustrated, they would probably begin to act out. She considered modifying the project to make it less complex, but she believed that backing down on rigor would cheat these same students of critical learning. Instead, she explained to the students that during the first few days of the project, she would be sitting on a stool in the middle of the room, a short, equal distance from each group, clearly visible to all students. Instead of moving around the room, her usual style, she would stay in the middle and students could come to her for help. From this strategic position, she could mentally shift her attention

from group to group, keeping each group in her sphere of attention so that she could monitor their progress. She found that in this way she was always ready to compliment specific examples of on-task behavior and to act quickly if it appeared that frustrations were going to lead to disruptions.

▶ **Observing a Master Teacher**

Of course, some aspects of withitness are quite subtle and situational. Over time, some teachers have developed these subtle aspects of withitness to a high degree. If you are having difficulty with withitness or simply want some new ideas, you can approach such a teacher and ask to visit her classroom simply to observe. After class, in a debriefing format, you would describe the behaviors that you noted that appeared to be particularly effective. A conversation with the mentor teacher should provide valuable insights about the types of things she looks for and the type of thinking she engages in when she senses potential problems. If you feel comfortable with the mentor teacher, you might invite her into your classroom to observe and provide recommendations. The following vignette depicts how this dynamic might play out in the classroom.

"The beauty of Mr. Killian's style of discipline is that it is done in a way that maximizes instructional time. As you watch him, notice the continuous flow of instruction." This is how the mentor focused the observation planned for Ms. Jacobson, a first-year teacher. Sure enough, as she sat in the back of the room, Ms. Jacobson observed Mr. Killian constantly moving throughout the room,

*always interacting with students about
the content. When he moved toward students who were beginning to disrupt, it
often appeared that he had been heading
in that direction anyway. His actions
were so subtle that they did not seem
threatening, yet any disruptive behavior
ended quickly. Ms. Jacobson wondered if
she would ever be able to perform such an
effective dance in her classroom. At least
now she had a clear model in mind, and
she knew that it was possible.*

ACTION STEP 2 ▼

*Employ specific techniques to maintain a
healthy emotional objectivity with students.*

Emotional objectivity involves an avoidance
of emotional extremes when dealing with students. This is especially important when you
are implementing negative consequences for
misbehavior like those described in Chapter 3.
At one extreme you might show anger when
disciplining students. A lesser but still ineffective reaction would be to show frustration
toward the student. Anger and frustration on
the part of a teacher are natural and sometimes unavoidable reactions to student misbehavior. But even if you do become angry
or frustrated, it is not useful to display
those emotions when employing negative
consequences.

Another emotion or disposition that
works against effective classroom management is hesitation. As Curwin and Mendler
(1988) note:

We have seen teachers who give consequences as if they are sorry that they

have to give them. These teachers are
telling students that they fear them and
the students learn quickly that this
teacher is easily intimidated. . . . On the
other hand, an overly aggressive deliv-
ery can create hostility, resentment, and
fear. These are not emotions that lend
themselves to setting up a growth-
producing interchange. (p. 98)

A number of specific techniques can help you
obtain and maintain a sense of emotional
objectivity with students.

▶ Looking for Reasons Why (Reframing)

Maintaining emotional objectivity is much
easier if you don't personalize student misbehavior. Even something as simple as trying to
understand the reasons why students mis-
behave can help you establish and maintain a
healthy objectivity. This is because misbehavior on the part of students usually has little to
do with a specific teacher (Dreikurs, 1968;
Dreikurs, Grunwald, & Pepper, 1982). Once
you realize this, you have a better chance of
depersonalizing student misbehavior. This
even works in the abstract. To illustrate, when
a specific student misbehaves, you can explicitly identify reasons why the student might
have misbehaved that do not imply disrespect
for or aggression toward you. This strategy is
a simple variation of a time-honored strategy
from clinical psychology sometimes referred
to as "reframing" (see Ellis, 1977; Meichenbaum, 1977). Langer (1989) exemplifies the
nature of reframing using the following
example:

. . . take a couple, Alice and Fred, whom
you see quite often. Sometimes you hear
them fight a bit. You don't pay any attention; don't all couples quarrel? Now you

learn that they are getting a divorce. You call to mind all the evidence that explains this outcome. "I knew it; [I] remember how they used to fight. Their fights were vicious." On the other hand, perhaps you hear that they have just celebrated their silver anniversary. "Isn't that nice," you say, "they have such a solid marriage; they hardly ever quarrel and when they do they always make up so sweetly to each other." (p. 64)

Langer's example depicts how we tend to reframe quite naturally and unconsciously. When done consciously to help maintain emotional objectivity toward a class or specific students, it might occur as depicted in the following vignette.

> *As a young man, Mr. Cannady used to experience road rage, feeling incredibly angry when other drivers did things like cutting him off or failing to yield. Then he took a course that taught him to use a technique called reframing. Now when someone cuts him off in traffic, he tells himself, for example, that the person is probably not paying attention because of a sick child and is trying to get home quickly. This new frame immediately calms him down and prevents him from feeling personally offended. When he began to teach, he transferred this technique to the classroom. When students refuse to do class work or if they talk back inappropriately or simply do not pay attention in class, Mr. Cannady tells himself that they are probably covering up insecurities, or that they must have had a bad morning at home, or that they just got some bad news. This approach helps Mr. Cannady keep calm and allows him to perceive students' behaviors as discipline challenges, not as personal attacks.*

▶ Monitoring Your Own Thoughts

One strategy for maintaining a healthy emotional objectivity involves taking the time to monitor your own attitudes about specific students (Good, 1982; Rosenshine, 1983; Rosenthal & Jacobson, 1968). This is similar to the strategy of reframing, but it has a different emphasis. You are probably aware that when your attitude about specific students is positive, it is fairly easy to interact with those students. However, you might not be aware of the extent to which negative attitudes toward specific students get in the way of interacting with them. The following process has been recommended to counteract the bias created by negative attitudes toward specific students (Marzano et al., 1997):

- Before class each day, mentally review your students, noting those with whom you anticipate having problems (either academic or behavioral).
- Try to imagine these "problem" students succeeding or engaging in positive classroom behavior. In other words, try to replace your negative expectations with positive ones.
- When you interact with these students, try to keep in mind your positive expectations.

The following vignette depicts how one teacher uses this process.

> *Ms. Young's mantra is "Don't hold a grudge." She desperately needs this mantra when she finds herself spending an entire evening obsessing about the behavior of a student that day. She understands herself well enough to know she must instead spend the evening saying*

over and over to herself, "Don't hold a grudge. Don't hold a grudge." Before she goes to bed, she also makes a commitment to herself that she will say three positive things to the student during the following two days. "Even if all I can find to compliment is the color of the students' clothes, I always find three things. The act of saying the positive things aloud changes my perceptions of that student, even if my positive statements are met with a scowl. By the time I have said the third positive thing, I almost always feel the tension in my shoulders ease, and I feel ready to develop a different relationship with the student. To paraphrase C. S. Lewis, I say the positive things not because it changes the students, but because it changes me."

▶ Taking Care of Yourself

The final strategy for maintaining a healthy emotional objectivity has nothing to do with students. Rather it has to do with taking care of your own emotional health. Curwin and Mendler (1988) explain the benefits of such behavior:

> We have stated time and time again that it is critical for you not to carry anger, resentment, and other hostile feelings once a discipline situation is over. If you are angry with a student from an incident that happened the day before, you might enter a power struggle just to flex your muscles and show who is boss. Don't. Start fresh each day. (p. 105)

Wisely they offer some simple suggestions for lessening the stress that might accumulate from a particularly difficult management day:

- Sit in a comfortable chair and practice deep-breathing exercises, keeping your mind free as you do so.
- Use guided imagery to create a "private retreat" for yourself that you visit briefly at the end of each day.
- Maintain a healthy sense of humor about your disciplinary encounters with specific students. Keep in mind that students are not adults yet and are acting out many issues that might have nothing to do with you.
- Seek out movies and television shows that make you laugh. Laughter is one of the easiest and most effective ways of lessening the tension that accompanies an unpleasant management experience.
- Be your own best friend by treating yourself to a reward on particularly difficult days.

The following vignette illustrates some of these techniques in action.

> *"It's no fun to teach anymore." Recently, Frank Catrera has noticed that he hears these words from colleagues more and more frequently. He feels sorry for them because he is still having a blast. Of course, he acknowledges that he also has dark days—there is no doubt about that. But whenever he notices that he is taking things too seriously, he knows what to do. Before going home, he goes into the media room to spend about 10 minutes watching his favorite video, an old, hilarious* Saturday Night Live *comedy sketch in which Jerry Seinfeld portrays a teacher with some very frustrating, but typical, students. No matter how many times he sees this tape, it always makes him laugh out loud. After hearing his*

colleague's comments, he decides that he probably needs to drag along a few of his colleagues with him next time, just to remind them teaching, even when frustrating, is fun.

Summary

The fourth aspect of effective classroom management, an appropriate mental set, involves two specific characteristics: withitness and emotional objectivity. Withitness is the ability to identify and quickly act on potential behavioral problems. Emotional objectivity is the ability to interact with students in a businesslike, matter-of-fact manner even though you might be experiencing strong emotions. This is particularly important to do when carrying out negative consequences for inappropriate behavior.

6

The Student's Responsibility for Management

Up to this point we have been considering actions a teacher can and should take regarding classroom management. Surely, the teacher is the guiding force in the classroom. But there is another side to the coin of classroom management, and that is the responsibility of students to contribute to the good functioning of the classroom. In fact, it is not uncommon for some theorists to react somewhat negatively to suggestions like those in Chapters 2 through 5. For example, in an article entitled "Discipline: The Great False Hope," Raymond Wlodkowski (1982) notes:

> Because discipline is so often applied as control, it comes across to the student as a form of direct or implied threat. We essentially say to the student, "If you don't do what I think is best for you to do, I am going to make life in this classroom difficult for you." (p. 8)

Jim Larson (1998) echoes this same sentiment, noting that "school disciplinary procedures . . . tend to rely more on reactive administrative interventions such as suspensions and expulsions. . . ." (p. 284). Larson offers a solution that involves students in the design and execution of management policies:

> A code of discipline specifies what would be considered appropriate school conduct and alleviates controversies associated with arbitrary rule enforcement . . . . Unlike, the older, legalistic code models with their heavy-handed authoritarian emphasis on rules and punishment, a modern code of discipline should be developed "bottom up" with collaborative input from students, teachers, support staff, and parents, and reviewed frequently for modification. (p. 285)

Larson goes on to explain that involving students in establishing and maintaining a well-run classroom has the effect of developing self-discipline and responsibility, which, he asserts, is ultimately, the most important benefit of such an approach. George Bear (1998) agrees, describing the positive consequences of fostering self-discipline in the following way: "Self-discipline connotes internal motivation for one's behavior, the internalization of democratic ideals, and is most evident when external regulations of behavior are absent" (p. 16).

As the preceding discussion and quotations illustrate, the terms linked with students' responsibility for their own behavior are many. They include *self-discipline, self-management, self-regulation, self-control, social skills,* and more. Regardless of the nomenclature used, the common theme running through all these discussions is that students should be given the message that they are responsible for their own behavior and that they should be provided with strategies and training to realize that control.

The Research and Theory

Ample evidence indicates that teaching responsibility is a high priority in U.S. education. Speaking of self-discipline, Bear (1998) explains that "the American public's belief that schools should play a role in teaching self-discipline has never been greater than it is today" (p. 15). He cites the 1996 Gallup study (Elam, Rose, & Gallup, 1996) indicating that 98 percent of the public believes that the primary purpose of public schools should be to prepare students to be responsible citizens.

The research on the impact of teaching students strategies geared toward personal responsibility is strong. Positive results using self-regulatory techniques range from increasing competence in specific academic areas (Stevens, Blackhurst, & Slaton, 1991) to increasing classroom participation (Narayan, Heward, Gardner, Courson, & Omness, 1990) to reducing behavioral problems (Charlop, Burgio, Iwata, & Ivancic, 1988).

The research on social skills training within the context of regular classroom management provides still another perspective on teaching responsibility. Specifically, teaching social skills focuses on providing students with strategies for controlling how they react to their peers (Cartledge & Milburn, 1978); Meadows, Neel, Parker, & Timo, 1991). Research shows that this ability is related to students' attitudes, their peers' attitudes about them, and academic achievement (Ciechalski & Schmidt, 1995; Green, Forehand, Beck, & Vosk, 1980; Vandell & Hembree, 1994; Weiner, Harris, & Shirer, 1990; Cain, 1990; Doughty, 1997; Larson, 1989; Wooster, 1986; Trapani & Gettinger, 1989; Hart, 1996). With this said, it is also important to note that a number of studies are able to establish a link between social skills and academic achievement (Robinson, 1985; Brickman, 1995; Dougherty, 1989; Fahringer, 1996; Kaufman, 1995; Bishop, 1989).

The results of my meta-analysis for student responsibility are reported in Figure 6.1. As indicated in Figure 6.1, the average effect size for teaching student responsibility strategies in general is −.694. This means that responsibility strategies are associated with a decrease of 25 percentile points in disruptive behavior. Note that Figure 6.1 also reports

Figure 6.1

Effect Sizes for Student Responsibility

	Average Effect Size	95% Confidence Interval	Number of Subjects	Number of Studies	Percentile Decrease in Disruptions
Responsibility Strategies (General)	−.694	(−.562) to (−.825)	1,021	28	25
Self-monitoring and Control Strategies	−.597	(−.408) to (−.786)	473	13	23
Cognitively Based Strategies	−.778	(−.479) to (−1.076)	203	5	28
High School	−.981	(−.574) to (−1.388)	109	3	34
Middle School/Junior High	−.826	(−.586) to (−1.066)	309	8	30
Upper Elementary	−.540	(−.348) to (−.733)	470	12	21
Primary	−.706	(−.339) to (−1.074)	133	5	26

effect sizes for two basic categories of responsibility strategies: *self-monitoring and control strategies* and *cognitively based strategies*.

Self-monitoring and control techniques are those in which students are taught to observe their own behavior, record it in some way, compare it with some predetermined criterion, and then acknowledge and reward their own success. I should note that some researchers refer to approaches within this category as contingency-based strategies, but I am using the term *self-monitoring and control* to avoid confusion with the group contingency–based strategies described in Chapter 3.

Cognitively based strategies also involve individuals observing and monitoring their own behavior. However, these strategies typically do not involve keeping a record of behavior, establishing a criterion level of

behavior, or rewards if the criterion is reached. Rather, cognitively based strategies involve examining one's thoughts as expressed in inner dialogue, considering the consequences of actions that are being considered along with alternative actions, and then selecting the most effective and positive course of action.

Despite strong research support for teaching responsibility strategies to students, it is apparently not done frequently in the context of K–12 education. In their review of the research, Edward Shapiro and Christine Cole (1994) explain:

Although educational personnel and parents alike agree that learning self-management skills is a priority for children, these skills are seldom systematically taught to students, especially those students with academic or behavior problems. The more typical emphasis has been on methods of classroom control and discipline using teacher-managed contingencies. (p. 2)

The lack of attention paid to developing students' responsibility for their own behavior is probably a function of the fact that addressing this issue typically goes beyond the traditional duties of a classroom teacher. As the Action Steps section of this chapter indicates, the interventions in this category generally are labor-intensive and supersede the type of relationship teachers typically form with their students and the students' parents and guardians. For these reasons, I have chosen not to list teaching responsibility as one of the defining elements of classroom management. Specifically, in Chapter 1, I listed four critical elements of classroom management: rules and procedures, disciplinary interventions, teacher-student relationships, and mental set. Obviously, teaching student responsibility is not on this list. This is not because it is ineffective. Indeed, Figure 6.1 attests to the power of directly addressing student responsibility. However, addressing student responsibility is a different order of magnitude than implementing rules and procedures, disciplinary interventions, and so on. It requires an extraordinary commitment—one that should be addressed thoughtfully. As Brophy (1996) explains, if teachers choose to address this realm, they should be willing to engage in the following actions:

1. Cultivate personal relationships with students that go beyond those needed for purely instructional purposes.

2. Spend time outside of school hours dealing with students and their families, without receiving extra financial compensation for your efforts.

3. Deal with complex problems that have developed over a period of years, without benefit of special training as a mental health professional.

4. Perhaps encounter some opposition from school administrators.

5. Perhaps encounter resentment or expressions of frustration from the students you are trying to help, their families, or others who may be involved in the situation. (p. 8)

I believe Brophy's comments are quite insightful and should be taken seriously before delving deeply into this domain. However, like Brophy, I encourage teachers to take on these added responsibilities.

Programs

A number of programs address various aspects of student responsibility. For example, the Child Development Project (Battistich, Watson, Solomon, Schaps, & Solomon, 1991) is one of the most promising for the development of self-regulatory skills. As described by Bear (1998), the Child Development Project is grounded in a cognitive-developmental, constructivist approach and focuses on the long-term development of pro-social behavior while de-emphasizing extrinsic control of rewards and punishments. Rather, it emphasizes the use of constructivist strategies for developing social responsibility, intrinsic motivation, and related pro-social behavior. However, it is only fair to comment that the program does employ traditional classroom management techniques such as the establishment and implementation of rules and procedures. It emphasizes resolving classroom conflicts using social problem-solving skills that have been developed in a constructivist atmosphere (i.e., students are encouraged to design their own strategies).

The Child Development Project includes a strong staff development component in which teachers receive about 30 days of inservice training over a three-year period. Relative to the effectiveness of the program, Bear notes:

> Program evaluations, which have included classroom observations, student interviews, and teacher rating scales, when compared to control groups have indicated that project children are more supportive, friendly, and helpful, and exhibit more spontaneous prosocial behavior. . . .
>
> Child interviews have indicated that project children have better social problem-solving skills as indicated on measures of social perspective taking . . . (pp. 24–25)

Other programs teach self-regulation and responsibility to young children. The Second Step Violence Prevention Program (Committee for Children, 1991) is one of these. According to Caroline Kelly (1997), the program helps children between the ages of 4 and 6 to learn pro-social skills and reduce impulsive behavior:

> The purpose of the program is to increase children's ability to identify others' feelings, others' perspectives, and to respond empathetically to others. Also, the program goals are to decrease impulsive and aggressive behavior in children by applying a problem-solving strategy to social conflicts, and to practice behavioral social skills. Recognizing angry feelings and using anger-

> reduction techniques help decrease angry behavior. (p. 27)

The components of the program include stories accompanied by discussion, role-playing activities, and lesson cards. These are supplemented by take-home activities that involve parents. To a great extent, children learn the importance of self-regulation skills and social skills by first learning about them through literature and then examining and practicing them.

Other noteworthy programs that directly or indirectly teach students responsibility for their own behavior include I Can Problem Solve (ICP) for primary and upper elementary students (Shure, 1992a, 1992b, 1992c); Think Aloud for primary and upper elementary students (Camp & Bash, 1985a, 1985b, 1985c); the Boy's Town Educational Model (Furst, Terracina, Criste, Dowd, & Daly, 1995; Doughty, 1997); and Goldstein and company's multicomponent social skills training program (Goldstein, Sprafkin, Gershaw, & Klein, 1980; McGinnis & Goldstein, 1984, 1990). For a review of these and others, consult Shapiro and Cole (1994) and Bear (1998).

ActionSteps

ACTION STEP 1 ▼

Employ general classroom procedures that enhance student responsibility.

A number of general practices foster students' responsibility for their own behavior and learning. These include classroom meetings, using a language of responsibility, written statements of belief, and written self-analyses.

▶ The Classroom Meeting

The classroom meeting is a powerful tool for teaching student responsibility (Glasser, 1969, 1986, 1990). Barbara McEwan, Paul Gathercoal, and Virginia Nimmo (1997) have articulated the following guidelines for effective class meetings:

- Determine who can call a class meeting and when it should be held according to standards of appropriate time and place.
- Seat students and teachers so that they can see the faces of all other class members.
- Establish the expectation that names will not be used in a class meeting because the purpose of class meetings is to address issues, not people.
- Establish the ground rule that the meeting will stay on topic.
- Establish the ground rule that students have the right not to participate in class meetings.
- Encourage or require students to use journals in conjunction with the class meetings. (pp. 31–33)

It is the last suggestion involving journals that teachers can use to great advantage in helping students to understand their own behavior. Specifically, you can ask or require students to keep a journal regarding the behavior of the class in general and themselves in particular. Every time you call a class meeting, you might ask students to make entries in their journals. Additionally, students might record

their thoughts and reactions in their journals at other strategic times—for example, when a disruption has occurred that is particularly upsetting to the smooth functioning of the class. The following vignette depicts how this might occur.

Ms. Dillon required her students to write in their logs after each of their class meetings. She noticed, however, that many students were struggling with this type of writing. Finally, after some trial and error, she provided a structure that helped. She asked students to draw a line down the middle of the paper. In the left column, they were to write a sentence or two describing each issue discussed at the meeting. In the right-hand column, across from each issue, they were to explain what was decided as a result of the class meeting, or at least how the discussion ended. Finally, across the bottom of the page, they were to write one or two sentences about how they felt about the meeting or one or two personal goals they had as a result of the discussion. When Ms. Dillon noticed the vast improvement in the log entries, she decided to start each meeting by asking several students to read what they had written after the previous meeting. This created accountability for the writing and gave the meetings continuity.

▶ A Language of Responsibility

The language we use is a window to our thoughts. Furthermore, linguists tell us that we develop a specific vocabulary for those things that are important to us. For example, if you grow up in a culture where snow skiing is important, you will develop a rich vocabulary regarding skiing and the types of snow to ski on (e.g., *parallel skiing, snow plowing, corn snow, powder, packed powder,* and so on) (see Lindsay & Norman, 1977; Pinker, 1994). This specialized vocabulary not only allows you to communicate better about skiing, but it also helps you understand skiing better. The same holds true for helping students develop responsibility for their own behavior—if they have no language to talk about responsibility, they have few tools with which to explore the concept. Consequently, Barbara McEwan, Paul Gathercoal, and Virginia Nimmo recommend beginning with a simple set of legal principles based on the Bill of Rights. This approach is referred to as "Judicious Discipline" (Gathercoal, 1993). Teachers using Judicious Discipline begin by introducing students to the basic concepts of rights, freedoms, and equality. This is followed by an explanation and discussion of the nature of these concepts within the classroom. To illustrate, McEwan, Gathercoal, and Nimmo (1997) comment on how the concept of personal freedoms might be addressed with students: "If a teacher, administrator, or staff member is able to demonstrate that the actions of students pose a threat to the health and safety, property, or educational purpose of the school, then students should have restrictions placed on their freedoms" (p. 4).

The centerpiece of the Judicious Discipline approach is the development of constitutional language that is used to discuss issues that arise in class. Again, McEwan, Gathercoal, and Nimmo (1997) explain: "When the language of citizenship, rights, and responsibilities is used to mediate problems between students and teachers, the classroom is transformed into a participatory democratic community" (p. 4). Critical terms that might be addressed when using this approach include *rights, freedoms, equality, responsibilities,* and *threats.*

Although the impact of Judicious Discipline on student behavior has not yet been well established, a number of studies have demonstrated that it alters the level of responsibility students take for their own actions (see Barr & Parrett, 1995; McEwan, Gathercoal, & Nimmo, 1997). The following vignette describes how a teacher might use this approach.

On the back wall of Ms. Lincoln's class was a bulletin board divided into three columns labeled as follows:

RIGHTS   RESPONSIBILITIES   REWARDS

From the first day, Ms. Lincoln told students that these were the most important three Rs in her class. Together as a class, they started to fill out the chart by identifying rights students should have in the classroom, the responsibilities students had to accept if they were to enjoy those rights, and the positive things that would happen if this balance of rights and responsibilities was maintained. For example, students said they had the right

- *To express their opinions,*
- *To walk around when they needed to, and*
- *To get help when they needed it.*

They then agreed that, with those rights, they had the responsibility to

- *Express opinions about ideas, not people,*
- *Move around the room without disrupting others, and*
- *Try to work independently before requesting help.*

The "Rewards" section listed ways that students would feel happier and learn better if they exercised each right and accepted the accompanying responsibility. Throughout the year at class meetings, students could propose adding rights to the list; however, they knew—because their peers reminded them—that they could not discuss rights without discussing the other two Rs.

▶ Written Statements of Beliefs

When we take time to articulate our beliefs, we are forced to be precise about those beliefs. Cecelia Netolicky (1998) describes an approach to developing student responsibility that relies heavily on the development of a document referred to as the "ethos document." This is because the term *ethos* means the *underlying beliefs and sentiments that inform the customs or practices in a group or a society.* Certainly a classroom represents a small society of sorts. The ethos document, then, contains assertions about the beliefs underlying the expected behaviors in the classroom. According to Netolicky, an ethos document typically contains statements like the following:

- All students have a right to be treated with respect.
- All teachers have the right to be treated with respect.
- Everyone has the right to feel safe in the teaching-learning environment.
- Students are expected to demonstrate a respect for the school's property.

Documents like the ethos document should be developed with thought and maximum input from students. This might be one of the first whole-class activities students

engage in at the beginning of the school year. The following vignette depicts how it might occur in the classroom.

Ms. Ramos kept thinking about what she had heard a judge say on her favorite TV crime-fighting program: "He might not have followed the letter of the law, but he certainly was true to the spirit of the law." That statement was bothering Ms. Ramos because it made her think that too much time was spent in her classroom negotiating with students about the "letter" of her rules, not about the spirit. The next morning she started class by writing on a piece of poster board: **The Spirit of the Rules.** *Underneath that title, she wrote,*

Everyone in this classroom . . .

She told her students about her experience with the television program the night before. "I decided that what was missing here was a common agreement as to the spirit of the rules, or, in other words, the motivation for the rules. We are going to do that now. I will go first." She wrote on the next line of the poster board.

. . . has the right to learn.

"I will go next," offered Sandra.

. . . should be able to be wrong without being embarrassed.

"I have two," Clarisse said.

. . . should do unto others as you would have them do unto you.

. . . feel accepted for who they are.

When they were finished, Ms. Ramos was thrilled with both the list and the process they had used to generate it. From that day on, when rules were mentioned for any reason, she always referred to the Spirit of the Rules list to guide their discussions and decisions.

▶ Written Self-Analyses

Along with the ethos document, Netolicky (1998) recommends that students use a prescribed form to record their analysis of behavioral incidents. She refers to this as the "self-defense" form. It includes the following elements:

- Date of the incident
- Location of the incident
- Others involved in the incident
- Student's response to questions like the following:
  - How I feel I contributed to the conflict
  - How I feel others contributed to the conflict
  - How I believe this should be resolved
  - How I can stop this from happening again
  - Final agreement relative to the incident

The basic purpose of the self-defense form is for students to articulate their perspective on a disciplinary incident in the context of a framework that requires them to examine their responsibility in the matter. Specifically, the questions that address how students contributed to the incident, how they can stop the incident from occurring again, and the agreements they are willing to make as a result of the incident are powerful stimuli to developing student responsibility. The following

vignette depicts how this might be apparent in the classroom.

The teachers at Campbell Middle School had heard about approaches to discipline that involved students in writing about behavioral incidents as a way of analyzing, and sometimes defending, their own role in the incidents. They were eager to develop a similar approach and began by creating the following sentence stems that students would complete as they analyzed their behavior:

I think that I contributed to the incident when I _____.

I think that _____ contributed when she/he _____.

I think the incident would not have happened if I had/had not _____.

I think the incident would not have happened if _____ had/had not _____.

When I think back on what happened, I wish _____.

Next time, if I am in a similar situation, I will _____.

I think the best solution to the problems caused by this incident is _____.

At first, teachers were pleased with their work, but then several teachers reminded the group that many of their students either had significant problems communicating in writing or had English language deficiencies that would make them extremely uncomfortable when trying to complete these sentence stems. Because they believed in the power of written self-analysis, they decided to keep working so that their format would work for all students. First, they set up a process that allowed students, when necessary, to respond to the sentence stems orally into a small cassette tape recorder. In this way, the teachers communicated to students that the self-analysis was more important than the writing. Second, the teachers translated the sentence stems into several languages, which helped to ensure that all students had the opportunity to analyze their behavior in the language with which they were most comfortable. When they finished the modifications, the teachers felt they had created a process that would provide opportunities for all students to analyze, and take responsibility for, their behavior.

ACTION STEP 2 ▼

Provide students with self-monitoring and control strategies.

As indicated in Figure 6.1, my meta-analysis focused on self-monitoring and control strategies and cognitively based strategies. Before considering the specifics of these strategies, it is worth recalling Brophy's (1996) caution that these techniques go above and beyond normal classroom practice and require an extraordinary commitment on your part. This said, they are probably among the most powerful things you can do to provide students with tools for the future. We begin with self-monitoring and control.

Self-monitoring and control strategies require students to observe their own behavior, record it in some way, compare it with some predetermined criterion, and then

acknowledge and reward their own success if the criterion is reached. Obviously this type of strategy cannot be employed with the entire class, nor should it be. Rather, it was designed to be used with specific students for whom general management techniques are not working.

Identifying students with whom you will use a self-monitoring and control strategy is usually straightforward. Candidates for self-monitoring and control are those students for whom other techniques you have tried simply have not worked. Obtaining agreement to use the strategy is not so straightforward. It usually requires a meeting or two with the student and ideally with his or her parents. One of the first things to establish in these meetings is that the student's behavior is a problem—not just for you but for the entire class and, ultimately, for the student. It is very helpful to have documented examples of the student's behavior and the impact of that behavior. Consequently, before the first meeting you might spend some time recording the specifics of the student's behavioral problems, perhaps over a week or two. Items you might record include the following:

• The date and time of the incident
• The context in which the incident occurred
• The specific actions of the student
• What you did
• The student's response to your actions
• The impact of the incident on the class, on you, and on the student

The next thing to establish with the student and the parents or guardians is that your intent is not to punish the student. To the contrary, your goal is to help the student succeed in your class and to provide the student with a strategy that can be used in a variety of situations. Such an interaction is fairly complex and should be approached with caution. The following vignette describes how this interaction might take place in the classroom.

> *Jason was a puzzle. Mr. Hancock had tried every strategy he knew to get Jason to stop disrupting class and to complete his work. What was most puzzling to Mr. Hancock, though, was knowing that Jason was a leader on his soccer team and had recently been selected as captain. Further, he knew Jason was bright, that when he applied himself he earned As and Bs. It was frustrating that Jason's missing work was destroying his record. This is the profile that Mr. Hancock presented during the meeting he set up with Jason, his parents, and the counselor. He began the meeting by placing two stacks of 3x5 cards on the table in front of them. On each card in one stack he had written a brief description of a wonderful trait that Jason had exhibited on good days. On each card in the other stack he had briefly described the kinds of disruptive behavior, referrals, and missing work that defined Jason on other days. "I want to figure out a way of removing this negative pile, leaving this positive pile as the one that describes Jason. What do you think, Jason? Will you work with me?" Jason hesitated, but did agree.*

Once a student has accepted the importance of self-monitoring and control strategies and your role as an advocate of good behavior, you can present a strategy to the student. There are a number of variations on self-monitoring and control strategies; however, they all follow a basic design. Below I present four generic phases of self-monitoring and

control. (For variations on this generic strategy, see Rhode, Morgan, and Young, 1983; Smith, Young, West, Morgan, and Rhode, 1988; and Shapiro and Cole, 1994.)

Phase I: Record Keeping and Contingent Rewards. In this phase, students periodically monitor their behavior. In the elementary self-contained classroom, this might happen every 30 or 45 minutes, given that teachers have students for most of the day or the entire day. In the middle school, junior high, or senior high class, this might be every 10 or 15 minutes, given that teachers generally have students for a single period only. Before establishing the record-keeping interval, you would have identified a specific behavior the student is trying to alter or stop. For example, the behavior for a given student might be talking to and trying to get the attention of nearby students. It is useful if you have established a cue to remind the student to record the behavior. That cue might be something as simple as tapping a certain part of your desk. Some teachers use a timer to remind themselves or the student that it is time to make a recording. At the appropriate times, the student would fill out a simple form like that shown in Figure 6.2. Notice that the scale in the figure moves from an unconscious repetition of the target behavior to a consciousness of it but no control over it, to a consciousness of it with some control, to a cessation of the behavior.

On a weekly basis (or less frequently), you and the student would establish target ratings on the record-keeping form. For example, the target for the first week might be for the student to have more ratings above 1 than ratings of 1. If the target is met, some reward is provided. Ideally the reward is something that the student has helped identify. Every

Figure 6.2
Student Self-Report Form

Time No. 1	1. I did it without even thinking about it.	2. I thought about it but still did it.	3. I thought about it and did it less than I normally would have.	4. I didn't do it.
Time No. 2	1. I did it without even thinking about it.	2. I thought about it but still did it.	3. I thought about it and did it less than I normally would have.	4. I didn't do it.
Time No. 3	1. I did it without even thinking about it.	2. I thought about it but still did it.	3. I thought about it and did it less than I normally would have.	4. I didn't do it.
Time No. 4	1. I did it without even thinking about it.	2. I thought about it but still did it.	3. I thought about it and did it less than I normally would have.	4. I didn't do it.
Time No. 5	1. I did it without even thinking about it.	2. I thought about it but still did it.	3. I thought about it and did it less than I normally would have.	4. I didn't do it.

week, more challenging targets are set. For example, the target for the second week might be more scores of 3 or 4 than scores of 1 or 2. Again, if the target is met, a reward is provided. This pattern continues until the student self-ratings are at a level acceptable to you and, ideally, the student.

Phase II: Monitoring Without Formal Record Keeping. In this phase, the formal record-keeping form is dropped and replaced by a less obtrusive method of record keeping. At first this might be written. For example, at the end of each day or each class, the student might summarize in writing how she felt she did relative to the target behavior. You might do the same. Over time the written summary

could be replaced by a verbal summary. You and the student would meet at the end of each week. If you both agree that the student's behavior was acceptable, then the student would receive the reward.

Phase III: No Formal Record Keeping, No Reward. In this phase, the student still keeps records in an informal manner, and you and the student still meet weekly to discuss the student's behavior. However, if you both agree that the student's behavior has been acceptable, no formal reward is given.

Phase IV: Student Autonomy. In this phase, the student has reached a level of autonomy. He does not have to meet with you to report on his behavior and to receive recognition or reward. However, you might still have occasional discussions with the student about his behavior.

The following vignette depicts how the self-monitoring and control process might occur in the classroom.

> *Whenever Mr. Hancock asked Jason why he disrupted class with his jokes and side comments, Jason always answered, "I don't know. I wasn't thinking, I guess." Mr. Hancock explained that he was going to set up the four-phase self-monitoring and control process to help Jason think. They began focusing on Jason's disruptive behavior. The plan was for Jason to carry a very small spiral notebook—small enough so that it could be slipped into one of the big pockets on the legs of his jeans—that Jason could use to keep track of his behavior. During class, Mr. Hancock regularly cued Jason to record the time and then to rate his behavior, using a coding system they had agreed upon (see Figure 6.2). As Jason left class each day, Mr. Hancock glanced at the ratings in Jason's notebook and, when appropriate, wrote a quick comment, such as "I hope tomorrow will be better" or "Kudos. Way to go."*
>
> *At the end of every two days, Mr. Hancock called Jason's parents with a report on how he was doing. If Jason met his goals, his parents provided concrete rewards (television time, instant-messaging time on the computer, etc.). Gradually Jason moved away from recording in his small notebook and simply discussed his progress with Mr. Hancock at the end of class. The phone calls home were less frequent, and the rewards became smiles and high-fives from Jason's parents. Interestingly, perhaps predictably, as Jason's disruptive behaviors decreased, his grades also improved.*

ACTION STEP 3 ▼

Provide students with cognitively based strategies.

As with self-monitoring and control strategies, a number of fairly specific cognitively based strategies have been devised (see Camp & Bash, 1985a, 1985b, 1985c; Goldstein et al., 1980; Goldstein & Pentz, 1984; Shapiro & Cole, 1994). For the regular classroom, these strategies fall under two broad categories: social skills training and problem solving. Social skills training involves providing students with strategies for handling social situations. These techniques are particularly useful for students whose lack of social skills creates discord in the classroom. For example, a student who has difficulty interacting with other students might cause a disruption in the classroom not because he wishes to violate classroom rules or procedures, but because he acts out his frustration due to poor interactions with other students. In Chapter 5, we referred to such students as socially inept. Problem-solving strategies are more generic in nature in that they are not geared toward social interactions only. Even though these two types of cognitively based strategies focus on somewhat different matters, they commonly employ the same process, which involves the following steps.

• **Step 1: Notice when you are becoming angry, annoyed, frustrated, or overwhelmed, and stop whatever you are doing.** Most often our emotions signal a pending problem before we are aware of it. Consequently, having students recognize their rising emotions is the first and probably most powerful step in cognitively based strategies. Along with this recognition, the students immediately stop what they are doing. The idea behind this is that actions under the influence of strong emotions are usually not well controlled or well thought out. Rather, they are simple reactions that are often negative in nature.

• **Step 2: Ask yourself, What are the different ways I can respond to this situation?** This second step has the potential to transform the student's actions from simple reactions to conscious decisions. Simply considering a number of possible responses to a given situation, whether it is a social situation (the student is having a disagreement with another student and becomes angry) or a more general problem (the student can't get the teacher's attention and becomes frustrated), shifts the realm of possibilities available to the student.

• **Step 3: Think about the consequences for each of your options.** The act of considering consequences places the student's action at a relatively high level of rational thought. It might appear that in a social or problem-solving situation students will not have a great deal of time to ponder consequences. However, the human mind is remarkably efficient at examining alternatives quickly (see Anderson, 1983, 1995). Consequently, even having a fleeting thought regarding the consequences associated with different alternatives is an effective deterrent to inappropriate behavior.

• **Step 4: Select the action that has the potential for the most positive consequences for you and others.** With alternatives considered, students are in a better position to select an appropriate course of action that has positive consequences for them and for other students. The logic underlying this step is that most people will select actions that are generally beneficial to themselves and others when they take the time to think about a situation and to examine alternatives and their consequences.

This cognitively based strategy can go a long way not only to help students change their behavior, but also to help them understand why and how they react to specific situations. Indeed, the simple act of stopping impulsive reactions puts students in a position to control their own behavior. The four steps described above have a broad range of applications. For younger students, the process might be presented in the following way:

1. When you feel like you might do something that is harmful, STOP and THINK.
2. What are some other things you can do?
3. What will happen if you do them?
4. Pick the best one.

To implement this cognitively based strategy, you would meet with the student and her parents or guardians and establish the fact that you are trying to help the student by presenting a strategy she can use. Considerable discussion would ensue about the specific behaviors the student would be working on. With cognitively based strategies, it is also important to model the type of thinking used in the steps described above. To do this you might "think aloud" as you walk the student through the process. For example, you would describe a situation in your life when it would have been appropriate to use the strategy. You would then go through each of the steps, describing your thinking as you do so. Next, you would identify a past situation in which the student could have benefited from the strategy. In this case you would ask the student to think through the steps, describing her thinking as she did so. Together you might brainstorm alternative actions she might have considered and the consequences for each. When students have had some practice using the protocol, they would then try it out in class.

It is useful to establish a cue that you can use to signal the student that it is a good time to use the cognitively based strategy. For example, with a student who has a problem with anger toward other students, you might establish the verbal cue of simply saying the student's name. The student would recognize this as your reminder that the strategy should be used at that particular moment. Periodically you would meet with the student to discuss how well the strategy is working. The following vignette describes how one teacher used the cognitively based strategy.

Ms. Overbey demonstrated the four-step process for "thoughtful behavior." To emphasize that process, she tried to illustrate the steps using pictures. She created a banner (Figure 6.3) and posted it across the top of the blackboard in her room. In addition to creating the class banner, Ms. Overbey printed mini-banners, just the right size for a bookmark. When she was working intensely with individual students, she gave them the bookmark as a personal reminder of the steps to thoughtful behavior. She often encouraged parents of disruptive students to reinforce the steps by discussing them at home.

One of her fondest memories was of Kayleen, a success story. The bookmark had not really been working until Kayleen herself developed a way of using it. Whenever Ms. Overbey noticed that Kayleen was getting angry, she would

Figure 6.3
Student Banner

Wait a minute! I'm feeling mad...

What should I do next? I could... or I could..

If I do that, then... But, if I....

I made the best choice!

give a cue to remind Kayleen to use her bookmark. Immediately, Kayleen would find her bookmark, lay it on her desk, place her fingers on the picture of the first step, close her eyes, furrow her brow, and think. She would then open her eyes, place her fingers on the second step, close her eyes, and think again. By the time she finished concentrating on each step, she was calm and determined to do the right thing. This would earn her a high-five from Ms. Overbey.

Summary

Although teachers are the guiding force in classroom management, students also have responsibility in this area. Working with students to develop this sense of responsibility requires an extraordinary effort and commitment on the teacher's part. However, useful strategies are available for teachers who want to help students make a significant contribution to the classroom management effort.

GETTING OFF TO A GOOD START

A classroom doesn't start off well managed. Rather, each year elementary teachers in self-contained classrooms meet with upwards of 30 new students who view the teacher as a new person in their lives. Secondary teachers might meet five or six new classes of students every semester—or even more frequently. Again, these students are as new to the teacher as the teacher is to them. For each of these fresh combinations of teachers and students, classroom management practices must be built anew. What, then, do we know about how an effectively managed classroom is first established?

The Research and Theory

A long history of research documents what we know about the beginning stages of developing an effectively managed classroom. Virtually all of this research points to the beginning of the school year as the linchpin

for effective classroom management. To illustrate, Moskowitz and Hayman (1976) studied the beginning-of-the-year behaviors of 14 highly effective junior high school teachers as compared with the behaviors of 13 first-year junior high school teachers. Where the new teachers spent relatively little time orienting the class to management routines and activities, the effective teachers not only focused the first few days on management, but they also did so in a very orderly and systematic manner—clearly articulating rules and procedures, practicing them with students, and establishing disciplinary consequences for violations of rules and procedures.

Researchers found similar results at the elementary level. In a study of 14 elementary school teachers identified as effective managers, Eisenhart (1977) found that the beginning of the school year was devoted to classroom physical arrangement, establishing a schedule of routines, and establishing a system of rewards and recognition. Buckley and Cooper (1978) reported that in effectively managed classrooms, teachers had firmly established management routines by the sixth day of class.

Perhaps the seminal studies on the beginning of the school year are a set of four conducted at the Research and Development Center for Teacher Education at the University of Texas at Austin. These were briefly discussed in Chapter 1. Two of these studies were at the elementary level and two were at the junior high level (see Emmer, Evertson, & Anderson, 1980; Anderson, Evertson, & Emmer, 1980; Evertson & Emmer, 1982; Sanford & Evertson, 1981; Emmer, Sanford, Clements, & Martin, 1982; Emmer, Sanford, Evertson, Clements, & Martin, 1981; Evertson, Emmer, Sanford, & Clements, 1983). Teachers were observed on the first day of class and then at regular intervals from one to two months later. Of the many findings, one of the more salient was that the most effective teachers not only planned for classroom management before actually beginning the school year, but they also spent more time ensuring that management activities were

- Understood by students,
- Generally accepted by students, and
- Practiced until they became routine.

Even if the research were not so clear, common sense dictates that devoting the first few days of the year, the semester, or the quarter to classroom management has the potential to ward off many future problems. Speaking about the secondary classrooms, Emmer, Evertson, and Worsham (2003) note, "The first few weeks of school are especially important for classroom management because during this time your students will learn behaviors and procedures needed throughout the year" (p. 58). Discussing the beginning of the school

year at the elementary level, Evertson, Emmer, and Worsham (2003) provide almost the exact same advice: "The beginning of the school year is an important time for classroom management because your students will learn behavior, attitudes, and work habits that will affect the rest of the year" (p. 58).

Programs

Most programs on classroom management pay some attention to the importance of the beginning of the school year. However, the Classroom Organization and Management Program, or COMP (see Evertson, 1995), addresses it quite directly and effectively. COMP was described in some depth in Chapter 2. Briefly, though, the program addresses seven specific elements of classroom management organized into the following modules:

1. Organizing the classroom
2. Planning and teaching rules and procedures
3. Developing student accountability
4. Maintaining good student behavior
5. Planning and organizing instruction
6. Conducting instruction and maintaining momentum
7. Getting off to a good start

The seventh module on getting off to a good start addresses the first few days of class and provides explicit guidance in how to introduce students to the critical features of the management system and how to do so in a way that involves students. The module on organizing the classroom provides specific suggestions regarding room arrangement, storage of equipment and material, and optimal design for whole-group and small-group discussion. All of these are key considerations that should be addressed at the beginning of the school year, semester, or quarter.

ActionSteps

ACTION STEP 1 ▼

Arrange and decorate your room in a manner that supports effective classroom management.

Although it might not be obvious, the way you arrange and decorate your classroom communicates a great deal to students, and the beginning of the year is the most powerful time to convey these communications. As Emmer, Evertson, and Worsham (2003) explain:

> Remember that the classroom is the learning environment for both you and your students. Although it may hold as many as thirty or more students each period, it is not a very large area. Your students will be participating in a variety of activities and using different areas of the room, and they will need to enter and leave the room rapidly when classes change. You will get better results if you arrange your room to permit orderly movement, few distractions, and efficient use of available space. (p. 2)

Emmer, Evertson, and Worsham (2003) and Evertson, Emmer, and Worsham (2003) make a number of general suggestions about classroom arrangement. I have combined theirs along with my own to produce the following list. Your classroom should be arranged in a way that allows all of the following:

- You can easily see all students.
- Students can easily see all presentations and demonstrations.
- Frequently used materials are easily accessible.
- Pathways facilitate traffic flow.
- It is easy to organize students into pairs, triads, and small groups.
- The room does not provide or highlight unnecessary distractions.

Figure 7.1 illustrates how an elementary classroom might be arranged. One of the first decisions you will have to make as an elementary teacher is where whole-group instruction will take place. Given that whole-class instruction should occur in a location where you can use the blackboard or white board, you might not have much of a choice on this issue. All students should be able to easily see this area without having to stand or move their chairs too much. As shown in Figure 7.1, you should have an overhead projector located in this area. Your desk should probably be located near the whole-class instruction area. This is particularly important if you use your desk as a storage place for materials that you use frequently during whole-group instruction.

You can arrange student desks and chairs in many ways. Notice that in Figure 7.1 the desks are organized in clusters as opposed to rows, yet all students can easily see the whole-class instruction area. Given the importance and frequent use of cooperative learning (see Chapter 2 for a discussion), the desk arrangement should allow you to easily organize students into groups of different sizes and different participants. The cluster arrangement in Figure 7.1 allows this.

Bookshelves should be located where they provide easy access but do not create traffic

Figure 7.1
Arrangement of Elementary Classroom

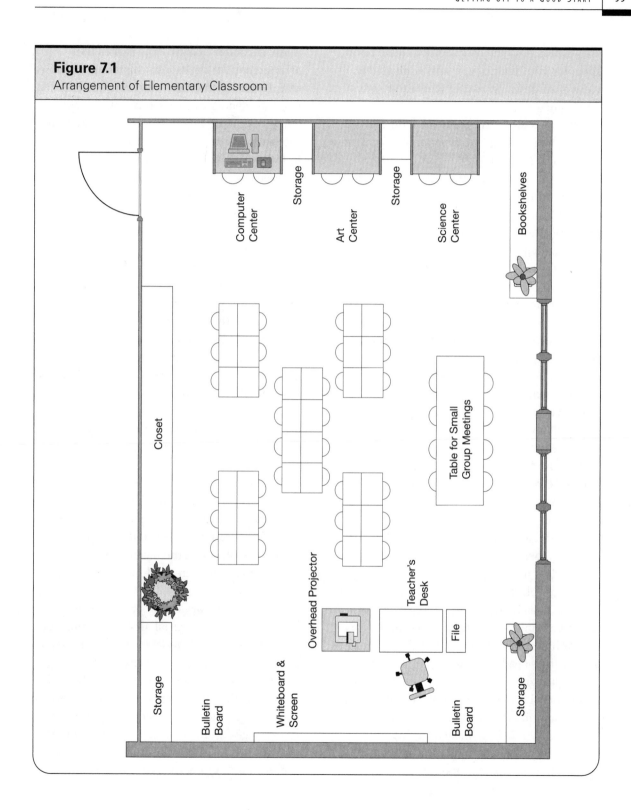

congestion. Also they should not create blind spots for you. That is, you will want a clear view of students no matter where they are in the room.

You will also want a place where you can meet with a small group of students (for reading groups, for example). Figure 7.1 shows a table on the right-hand side of the classroom (looking from the area for whole-class instruction). When you are interacting with a small group of students, your chair should be placed with its back to the wall so that you can see the entire class.

Many elementary classroom teachers use centers—places where students come together to work on specific projects or to study a specific topic. At the elementary level, students commonly go to centers for art and science activities. Again, these centers should be located away from major traffic patterns but in places you can easily see and monitor. Ideally, you will have a computer or computers in your classroom with access to the Internet. Your computer area might be thought of as another center. The materials necessary for use in the centers should be located close by.

Figure 7.2 shows a possible arrangement for a secondary classroom. Again, one of the first decisions you will want to make is where whole-class instruction will take place. Easy access to a blackboard or white board is again important, as is an overhead projector and an accompanying table. All students should have a clear line of vision to you, the blackboard, and the overhead projector.

Although there are many ways to arrange student desks, many secondary teachers still prefer organizing students in rows as depicted in Figure 7.2. This makes it a little more difficult to quickly organize students into cooperative groups, but the class size in many secondary classrooms makes the arrangement of desks into clusters prohibitive. Ensuring that desks are not too close together decreases the chances of students being distracted by one another. Notice that the teacher's desk is in the back of the room in Figure 7.2. Although it is certainly appropriate to place the desk in the front of the room near the whole-class instruction area, placing it at the opposite end of the room from where whole-class instruction takes place ensures that you will often be both at the back and the front of the room. Also, placement of your desk at the back of the room allows you to observe students doing seatwork without them knowing exactly what part of the room you are observing.

Again, a place should be set aside for groups of students to meet or for you to work with small groups. In Figure 7.2, the small-group area is located on the left-hand side of the classroom looking from the perspective of the location for whole-class instruction.

Secondary classrooms typically do not have centers, but you will ideally have a computer or computers in the classroom with access to the Internet. These should be placed away from traffic patterns but in a spot where students working at them can be seen. Storage space for computer-related materials should be close by.

Some secondary classrooms—science classrooms and industrial arts classrooms, for example—are set up as laboratories. The same considerations apply to lab environments, although you probably will have less flexibility with seating arrangements given the permanent nature of the equipment in these spaces.

Along with the physical arrangement of the room, you should consider how the room is decorated. Again, the physical appearance

Figure 7.2
Arrangement of Secondary Classroom

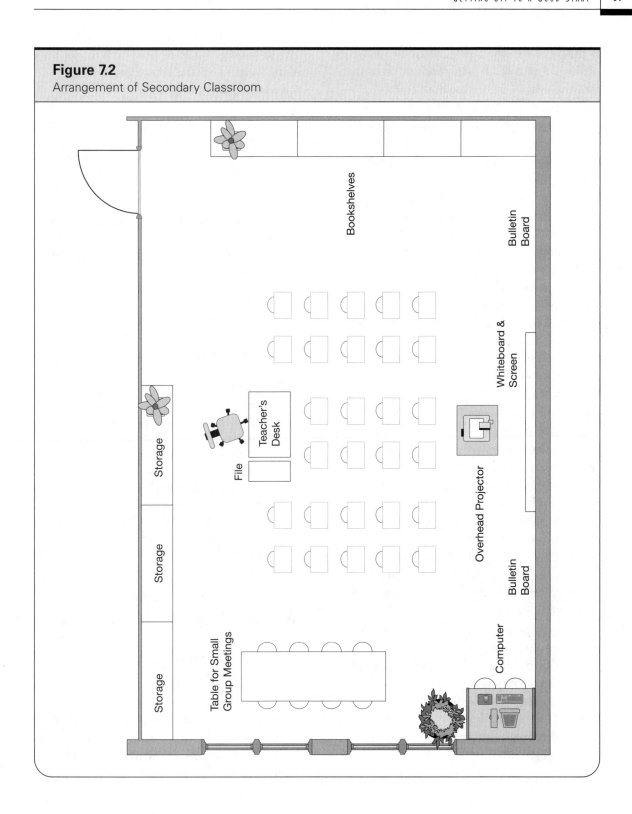

of the room conveys a powerful message when students first enter. It is important to note that the emphasis in decorating the classroom should be on functionality. That is, it is not your job to create a "pretty" environment; it is your job to create a "learning" environment. As Evertson, Emmer, and Worsham (2003) explain, "Don't spend a lot of time decorating your room. You will have many other important things to do to get ready for the beginning of school. A few bare bulletin boards won't bother anybody" (p. 5). With this important qualifier in mind, I offer some suggestions for decorative elements that are commonly employed in effectively managed classrooms.

An elementary classroom may include the following decorative elements:

- A calendar
- A place for school announcements and school spirit paraphernalia
- A place for posting expectations regarding the correct format for assignments (e.g., the proper format for headings on papers)
- A place for listing daily assignments or the daily schedule
- A place for displaying information about current topics
- A poster with a pocket for each child that can be made of laminated envelopes. These pockets can be used to send messages to individual students.

A secondary classroom may include the following decorative elements:
- A place for school announcements and school spirit paraphernalia
- A place where school assignments can be listed
- A place to display prototypes for assignments
- A place to display student work

The following vignettes describe how teachers at the elementary and secondary levels approached decorating their rooms.

- *Ms. Rice used to spend several days before school started decorating her classroom. Not any more. Now the kids arrive to an almost bare classroom, and then she and the kids decorate the walls. Together they put up calendars, frame areas for students' work, and create individual spaces for their personal materials. As they work, Ms. Rice explains the purpose and value of each space. She is convinced that by doing this they understand and use the resources in the spaces much more quickly. She now uses more of the time before school starts for curriculum planning.*
- *For his first two years of teaching, Mr. Crank had to admit his computer lab deserved the reputation of "drab lab." He wanted to decorate but hated spending time on it. Of course, he finally realized that the technology around him could solve the problem for him. With software he knew well, he created amazing calendars, assignment boards, and reminders—all in the school colors. The best brainstorm idea he had, however, was a "virtual" bulletin board that he periodically projected on the ceiling.*

ACTION STEP 2 ▼

Begin with a strong first day of class.

The frequently used expression "you have only one chance to make a first impression" applies well to the first day of class. What you do that first day sets a tone that can carry you through the rest of the year. There is no set pattern to the activities you should engage in, but there are some general suggestions that seem to work. Again, I have combined the suggestions of Emmer, Evertson, and Worsham (2003) and Evertson, Emmer, and Worsham (2003) with some of my own.

In the elementary classroom, here are some critical things to do on the first day of class:

• Prepare student name tags, but have extra material available in case new students are assigned to class.

• When students enter the room, greet them warmly and help them put their name tags on and be seated. Alternatively, you might tape their name tags to their desks.

• Make a seating chart.

• Don't allow students to wander around or become confused.

• Tell students something about yourself and have them do a brief get-acquainted activity. For example, you might have students tell their name and a favorite activity or use a name game to help students remember each others' names. You might also ask them to complete a brief interest inventory like the one shown in Figure 7.3.

• Present and discuss the classroom rules and procedures along with the disciplinary interventions.

The following vignette illustrates how the first day of class might play out in an elementary classroom.

The first day of school, Mr. Jake greeted every student with a name tag. Beside each student's name on the tag were several stickers symbolizing some aspect of the curriculum—an animal, a shape, a letter, a story title. Throughout the day, Mr. Jake grouped and regrouped students according to one of the symbols. ("Okay, we're going to group by animals. Everyone with a dog, get together here; everyone with a bird . . . .") During each grouping, students first got acquainted, and then Mr. Jake gave them information and opportunities to discuss ideas about both the

---

Figure 7.3

An Interest Inventory for Elementary Students

1. What kind of pet do you have? If you don't have a pet, what kind would you like to have?_____

_____

2. What is your favorite subject in school? _____

3. Why? _____

4. What is your favorite TV show? _____

5. What do you like to do after school? _____

curriculum goals and the class routines. By the end of the day, every student had been grouped with every other student, and Mr. Jake had introduced the curriculum.

At the secondary level, here are some actions to take on the first day:

• Before class begins, stand near the door. Monitor the general activity in the hallways and help students in the hallway find their way to their classes.

• As students enter your classroom, greet them. Explain that for this first day they will be allowed to select their own seats, but you will assign seats at a later date.

• Begin class by addressing any required administrative tasks such as roll call and filling out forms or cards for the central office. As students fill out the forms or cards, have them hold them up so that you can collect them.

• Tell students your name and something about yourself, such as your family background, your teaching experience, your hobbies, and so on. If students don't know each other, provide them with a brief get-acquainted activity. For example, you might organize students in triads and ask each student to say their name and something about themselves. At this point you might also have students fill out an interest inventory like that in Figure 7.4.

• Provide students with a brief activity that conveys a sense of the content you will be addressing and the type of activities they will be engaged in.

• Give students a course outline and briefly go over your expectations. (This is not the time to provide in-depth explanations of assignments or grading criteria.)

• Give students a written copy of the rules and procedures for the class along with

---

Figure 7.4
An Interest Inventory for Secondary Students

1. What is your favorite subject in school? _____

2. Why? _____

3. What do you like to read about? _____

4. What is your favorite book? _____

5. What is your favorite movie or television show? _____

6. What would you like to do after you graduate from high school? _____

_____

7. What are your hobbies? _____

your system of negative and positive consequences. Go over them, explaining the rationale for each one. Allow students to ask questions, and explain that they will have an opportunity to alter the rules and procedures.

• End the period with an end-of-class routine that ensures that materials are put away and the room is left clean.

The following vignette depicts the first day of class in a secondary classroom.

> *Mr. Ames decided to try something new with his sophomores, knowing that many of them were weary of the first-day-of-school lectures and routines. As they walked in, he immediately put them in small groups. Before each major chunk of information he provided, he asked them to predict what he was going to say—about himself, his grading policies, the curriculum, and so forth. The groups whose predictions were closest to the actual information won points toward the prize—a giant chocolate bar. Mr. Ames then proceeded to describe his background. Given that many of the students didn't know each other, he had them fill out an interest inventory, and then he organized them into triads and asked them to share some information about themselves. Next, he briefly went over the rules and procedures that would be employed. He invited questions and concerns from students and explained that these issues would be addressed another day. Finally, he provided a brief summary of the curriculum and his expectations, again noting that he would address concerns and questions later. At the end of the period, he concluded that students were actually listening to the details of his information—plus they were thinking on the first day of school.*

ACTION STEP 3 ▼

Emphasize classroom management for the first few days.

Within the first week or so, your management system should be well established. This requires a number of activities. At the elementary level, some of them are the following:

• Introduce new students to the class, taking time to help other students learn something about the new student.

• Practice the classroom routines with students until they can execute them efficiently and without confusion.

• Go over the classroom rules and procedures that were presented the first day and the disciplinary interventions that accompany them. Spend time discussing the rationale for them and invite discussion and input from the students. If necessary, make changes in the rules, procedures, and disciplinary interventions that reflect the strong sentiments of the students.

• Set up a system for communicating with parents.

• Go over the grading procedures you will be using. Again, invite discussion and input from students.

• Continue to engage in activities that allow students to get to know you better and to get to know one another better.

The following vignette depicts how some aspects of the first few days of class might play out in an elementary classroom.

> *"Freeze! Now, pair up with the person next to you, make sure you know each other's name, and talk about the rules and procedures that you should be following*

right now. Then give yourself and the whole class a score from 1 through 4 (4 is the highest) to rate how well we are following the rules."

Ms. Winger uses this little "freeze" activity with her 1st graders several times during the first week of school to reinforce rules and procedures at the exact moment they need to be followed. If she senses that students are confused, she takes the time to review the specific rule or procedure with them. She also uses these times to explain and discuss with students why the rules and procedures are important.

At the secondary level, activities to engage in during the first few days of class include the following:

- Introduce new students to the class.
- Spend time going over the rules and procedures and accompanying disciplinary interventions. Explain their rationale and invite input from students. Make changes that reflect the strong values of students.
- Review the classroom routines you have established (e.g., beginning of class, ending the class, passing out material, working in groups, and so on). If necessary, practice some of these routines.
- Make a concentrated effort to memorize the names of each student and learn something about each student.
- Go over your grading procedures in depth. Invite input and discussion from students.

The following vignette depicts how some aspects of the first few days of class might play out in a secondary classroom:

Although Ms. King did not assign academic homework on the first day of school, she did ask students to prepare a 10-question quiz—including questions on the information she presented about the classroom rules and procedures, and 2 questions that asked for information about the students and their interests. For the next two days, during the first few minutes of class, each student circulated and randomly gave their quiz orally to several other students. In this way, they got to know each other, as well as the rules. After a few rounds of questions, she invited the whole class to comment on their perceptions regarding the effectiveness and fairness of the rules and procedures. Given that each student had considered the rules and procedures in depth, the discussion was lively and productive.

Summary

The beginning of the school year is the critical time to set the tone for classroom management. Such things as room arrangement and decoration provide a subtle but important communication to students regarding how you will manage the classroom. The first day of class provides an important opportunity to make a good first impression and to introduce rules and procedures that will form the basis for your classroom management routine. Reinforcing students' understanding of the rules and procedures through various activities during the first few days of the school year will help ensure that your classroom management procedures are well established.

8
MANAGEMENT AT THE SCHOOL LEVEL

Chapters 2 through 5 addressed actions that individual teachers can (and should) take to manage their classrooms. Chapter 6 considered ways to help students take responsibility for their own behavior, and Chapter 7 addressed ways to begin the year so that classroom management gets off to a good start. This chapter addresses those actions that the school can take. Although this might sound like a change of topic, it is not. School-level management and classroom-level management have a symbiotic relationship that is probably best understood if we consider the perspective of an individual student.

Cecilia, a middle school student, attends five classes a day, each taught by different teachers. Each teacher employs specific management techniques, and their management skills will give Cecilia a sense of safety and order in these classes. However, she is not in class the entire school day. She goes to lunch; she walks through the hallways between classes; she spends time in common areas used by all students, and so on. An effectively managed school from the perspective of Cecilia, then, is not only what she experiences from individual teachers, but what she experiences from the school during those activities and in those places that all students share. If we consider this aspect of effective management in conjunction with the classroom management techniques discussed in Chapters 2 through 7, we see that effective management is a composite of interacting elements. Figure 8.1 illustrates this interaction.

As shown in Figure 8.1, school-level management provides the larger context in which classroom management takes place. This makes intuitive sense because the school establishes the overall environment in which individual classrooms operate. It is the combined impact of the effective management of

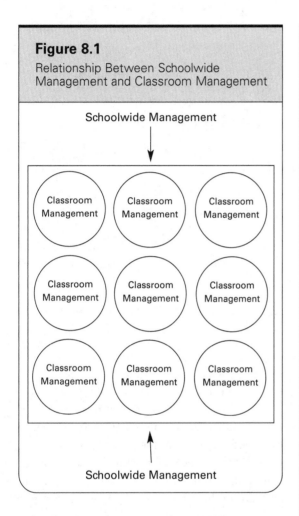

Figure 8.1
Relationship Between Schoolwide Management and Classroom Management

Schoolwide Management

Classroom Management

Classroom Management

Classroom Management

Classroom Management

Classroom Management

Classroom Management

Classroom Management

Classroom Management

Classroom Management

Schoolwide Management

individual classrooms and the school as a whole that constitutes a student's perception of the school.

The Research and Theory

A well-managed school is so important to the achievement of students that is has been identified as a national goal. Specifically, the Goals 2000: Educate America Act (National Education Goals Panel, 1994) stated that by the year 2000, every school "will offer a disciplined environment conducive to learning" (p. 13). However, even with this impressive endorsement, individual classroom teachers do not necessarily view schoolwide management as within the scope of their responsibilities. This observation was the impetus for a review of the research conducted by Kristine O'Brien (1998):

> When I finished my student teaching in the fall of 1997 at [a middle school] in central Virginia, I left wondering why teachers allowed students so much freedom to misbehave in the hallway. In the classrooms, teachers were firmly in charge: students knew the rules and knew that breaking them would bring consequences. The hallways were another story entirely. My first week at [the school], I felt ill at ease as I heard muttered curse words, saw a lot of playful but rough physical contact between students, and watched students running and jumping to touch the ceiling. Sometimes teachers reprimanded students, but often the behavior was let go. By the end of my eight-week teaching experience, I was able to ignore the rather wild atmosphere, only getting involved when it seemed a fight might break out. (p. 4)

O'Brien goes on to say that "the teachers were not oblivious of the dichotomy between hall and class behavior standards; I often sensed frustration about student behavior and confusion about when to intervene, but no one discussed it or looked for solutions" (p. 5).

Ample evidence suggests that poor management at the school level communicates a strong counterproductive message to students. Speaking of violence in particular,

Carole Rembolt and Richard Zimman (1996) explain: "By tolerating violence, we're telling students who feel entitled to be violent that we agree with them. Their attitude of entitlement and our attitude of tolerance toward it, are part of the enabling system" (p. 46). Rembolt and Zimman go on to explain that a school communicates tolerance for misbehavior at the school level when teachers or administrators engage in the following behaviors:

• Failing to set clear, consistent standards of school conduct
• Purposely avoiding areas of the building or grounds where students are known to act aggressively
• Not intervening when a student commits a violent act or disruptive act or threatens to do so
• Not reporting violence and verbal threats of aggression
• Not reporting rumors of planned fights on or off the school grounds
• Pretending not to notice threats and acting out in the classroom and hallways
• Failing to report complaints from victims of aggression (p. 55)

In their book, *Rethinking Student Discipline: Alternatives That Work,* Paula Short, Rick Short, and Charlie Blanton (1994) note that the laissez-faire approach of some teachers to school-level management is probably a function of certain attitudes that include the following:

• The "He's Not My Student" Syndrome or the teacher who ignores misbehavior of students.

• The "I'll Keep a Low Profile" Syndrome or the teacher who is present in body but not in mind.
• The "It's None of My Business" Syndrome or the teacher who tries to become an ally of the student by subtly telling the student, "I'll stick to my business, you stick to yours." (p. 12)

In addition to the clear pragmatic reasons why management at the school level should be addressed directly, there are also public relations reasons. A great deal of evidence shows that the public at large judges the effectiveness of a school in terms of its management of student behavior. To illustrate, safety in schools appears to be a major concern of parents (see Coldron & Boulton, 1996). Polls at the national and local levels consistently demonstrate that the general public perceives safety as one of their primary issues (Sewall & Chamberlin, 1997). As Pedro Noguera (1995) notes: "In many school districts concerns about violence have even surpassed academic achievement—traditionally the most persistent theme on the nation's agenda—as the highest priority for reform and intervention" (p. 189). It is important to mention that the perceptions regarding the lack of safety in U.S. schools might exceed the reality. For example, commenting on the perceptions of safety in the San Antonio, Texas, public schools, Leal (1994) notes, "Reading the city's major newspaper, one might get the impression that many school children are involved in crime and drugs. However, the reality is much different" (p. 39).

Similarly, as a consequence of a poll they conducted, Phi Delta Kappa and the Gallup organization cautioned that the perceptions of violence might be more a function of extensive media coverage than of actual incidents of school violence (Miller, 1994). Finally, Noguera (1995) explains that "relatively speaking, young people may, in fact, be far safer in school than they are in their neighborhoods or, for that matter, at the park, the roller rink, or even in their homes" (p. 191).

There is even some evidence that public concerns about violence in schools have been used as a political tool. For example, Sewall and Chamberlin (1997) explain:

> There has also been the suggestion that the perception of school violence has been politicized. As the attitude of the public has become more harsh toward the incidence of crime and general lawlessness, there has been a tendency on the part of elected officials and school boards and administrators to adopt a "get tough" policy to convince the public that appropriate action is being taken. (p. 4)

With these qualifications noted, the data regarding misbehavior and violence in schools are still sobering. For example, in the late 1990s, a spokesperson for the American Federation of Teachers reported that 1 out of 11 teachers is assaulted in schools and 1 out of 4 students experiences violence in schools. At the same time, the executive director of the National School Safety Center noted that an estimated 5,000 teachers are assaulted each month. Of these, about 1,000 are injured seriously enough to require medical attention (in Ward, 1998).

Data obtained from and about students are equally sobering. In a survey of 2,066 9th grade students in Lexington, Kentucky, during a sixth-month period, 43 percent of the students reported that they had hit another student, 8 percent reported that they had hit a teacher, and 16 percent reported that they had carried a weapon to school (Kingery, McCoy-Simandle, & Clayton, 1997). In a survey of a representative sample of high school students in Seattle, 6.6 percent reported that they had carried a handgun to school at some time (Callahan & Rivera, 1992).

Even if the incidents of misbehavior and violence are not any greater than they were in previous years, the negative impact of this behavior in schools is well documented. For example, in a study that controlled for background characteristics such as race/ethnicity and socioeconomic status, students in schools with high levels of violence had lower math scores by .20 of a standard deviation and were 5.7 percentage points less likely to graduate than students in schools with relatively little violence (Grogger, 1997).

In short, an emphasis on the effective management of the school in general is as important as individual classroom management and may even be a bigger determinant of the climate of the school than the aggregate impact of the management in individual classrooms.

ActionSteps

ACTION STEP 1 ▼

Establish rules and procedures for behavioral problems that might be caused by the school's physical characteristics or the school's routines.

The old saying that "an ounce of prevention is worth a pound of cure" applies nicely to schoolwide management. The more attention a school pays to rules and procedures regarding its physical environment and routines, the fewer chances there are for disruption and misbehavior. J. Ron Nelson, Ron Martella, and Benita Galand (1998) refer to such rules and procedures as "ecological interventions." For example, in a four-year study involving about 600 students in grades 1 through 6, they found that

> . . . having students of similar grade levels participate in a recess period created congestion problems because same-age students tended to participate in the same activities. This led to more physical and undesirable social interactions among students. Mixing up the grade levels during the recess periods reduced the congestion problems. (p. 155)

Ecological interventions, then, are rules and procedures that counteract possible negative consequences of the school's physical characteristics (e.g., narrow hallways, limited access to and from certain areas) or of the school's schedule (e.g., overlapping lunch periods, staggered schedules). To implement ecological interventions, a school must examine its physical structure and routines with an eye to heading off possible problems. Ecological interventions recommended by Nelson and his colleagues include these:

- Reducing the density of students by using all entrances and exits to a given area
- Keeping to a minimum wait time to enter and exit common areas

- Decreasing travel time and distances between activities and events as much as possible
- Controlling physical movement by using signs marking transitions from less controlled to more controlled space
- Controlling behavior by using signs indicating behavioral expectations for common areas
- Sequencing events in common areas to facilitate the type of behavioral momentum desired

Once a school has identified the need for an ecological intervention, Nelson and his colleagues recommend that the school employ a three-phased approach to teach and reinforce the relevant rules and procedures. During the first phase, students are taught the rules and procedures for the common areas. This might take two to three weeks. In the second phase, students receive periodic reviews of those rules and procedures. This might last from two to three months. In the third phase, students receive review sessions or "booster sessions" as needed. The following vignette depicts how a school might approach ecological interventions.

The principal of Mission School sat in her office examining the reports of incidents and injuries that occurred in the hallways of her school that year. Most of the problems occurred on the narrow wooden stairs and ramps of the old school building. Because of the unusual placement of these stairs, they often became clogged when some students tried to go up the stairs while other students were coming down. She smiled as she remembered the old movie Up the Down Staircase. As she pondered the problem, she noticed a brightly colored image on her computer screen. She had an idea. With cooperation from the maintenance department and volunteer parents, some sets of stairs were painted a special shade of yellow, called buttercup. Other stairs were painted a light brown. After the new paint job, the principal launched an informational campaign to make sure all students knew the new rules, represented in the slogan: "Buttercup is up; brown is down." The school held an assembly, all classroom teachers reinforced the new procedures, and the slogan was repeated whenever necessary. The color coding was so successful that the principal also had the landings of the staircases painted bright red, meaning students needed to keep moving. A new slogan was born: "No parking in red zones." In fact, red paint was used on all areas of the school where loitering caused problems. Some teased the principal about her color coding, but everyone agreed that it helped reduce the number of problems in these areas of the school.

ACTION STEP 2 ▼

Establish clear schoolwide rules and procedures regarding specific types of misbehavior.

Just as it is important to establish rules regarding specific types of misbehavior at the individual classroom level, so, too, is it important to establish rules and procedures regarding specific types of misbehavior at the school level. A study of referrals involving 11,000 students in 19 middle schools provides an interesting perspective on the frequency of various types of schoolwide misbehavior that warrant referrals. Study authors Russell Skiba, Reece Peterson, and Tara Williams (1997) report that

- 41.1 percent of the students had one or more referrals for misbehavior; and
- Those students who were referred averaged 3.77 referrals per year (p. 299).

Specific types of misbehavior that lead to a referral are reported in Figure 8.2. As the figure indicates, disobedience, classroom interference, and disrespect account for more than 50 percent of the reasons for referrals. One of the more interesting aspects of Figure 8.2 is that the more severe forms of misbehavior such as obscene language, endangering others, and abusive language are relatively rare. Additionally, criminal misbehavior is even more rare. In fact, in the Skiba, Peterson, and Williams study, use of weapons accounted for only .1 percent (21 of 17,045 incidents) of the incidents of misbehavior, theft only .9 percent (146 of 17,045 incidents), and drug or alcohol possession only .2 percent (32 of 17,045 incidents).

The findings of the Skiba, Peterson, and Williams study, which was conducted at the middle school level, are fairly consistent with the findings of studies that have been conducted at other grade levels (see Bear, 1998; Billings & Enger, 1995; Green & Barnes, 1993). Combining the findings of the research on schoolwide misbehavior produces a comprehensive list of behaviors:

- Bullying
- Verbal harassment
- Use of drugs
- Obscene language and gestures
- Gang behavior

Figure 8.2
Top 10 Reasons for Referrals

Behaviors	Percentage	Cumulative Percentage
Disobedience	27.6	27.6
Classroom Interference	12.8	40.4
Disrespect	10.7	51.1
Fighting	10.6	61.7
Excess Noise	6.0	67.7
Abusive Language	5.0	72.7
Miscellaneous	4.8	77.5
Endangering Others	3.6	81.1
Obscene Language/Gestures	3.0	84.1
Tardiness	2.7	86.8

Source: Adapted from Russell Skiba, Reece Peterson, and Tara Williams. Office referrals and suspension: Disciplinary interventions in middle schools. *Education and Treatment of Children, 20*(3), 295–315. Copyright 1997. Education and Treatment of Children.

- Sexual harassment
- Repeated disruption of classes
- Disregarding the safety of others
- Fighting
- Theft
- Truancy

As with ecological interventions, rules and procedures regarding specific types of misbehavior such as these should be clearly communicated to students and made highly visible. Common approaches are to review schoolwide rules and procedures at the beginning of the school year, perhaps in an assembly, and provide students and parents with a written copy of those rules and procedures. The school might also schedule an open house night for parents who have questions about the schoolwide rules and procedures. The following vignette depicts how a school might communicate schoolwide rules and procedures to students.

Every room in Ranch Middle School was equipped with a large TV monitor that was wired to a central network. In addition, the district had a new technology director who was known for using technology in creative ways. Everyone was aware that he was a fan of old movies and had an extensive library of movie clips. With the aid of the technology director, the principal devised a new approach to presenting schoolwide rules and procedures. The technology director helped him craft a very creative PowerPoint presentation, interspersed with relevant movie clips, to explain and highlight each rule and procedure. Students paid close attention during the presentation about rules for the cafeteria, media centers, hallways, and breaks. Consequences for violating school policies were clearly explained and illustrated in creative, often humorous ways. Because the presentation was on the school network, teachers could pull up segments and review the rules with students at appropriate times. Additionally, the presentation could be used with parents during conferences and back-to-school nights.

ACTION STEP 3 ▼

Establish and enforce appropriate consequences for specific types of misbehavior.

Identifying specific types of misbehavior is only one part of the equation for an effectively managed school. A school must also establish consequences for misbehavior that are fair and consistently administered. Research indicates that the types of consequences used by schools seem to be fairly consistent. Again, the study by Skiba, Peterson, and Williams (1997) provides an interesting perspective. The 10 most frequently employed consequences for referrals at the school level are listed in Figure 8.3.

As the figure shows, home suspension is the most common consequence of a referral. Home suspension, reprimand, and in-school

suspension account for more than 55 percent of the total consequences. What is not reported in Figure 8.3 is that corporal punishment was employed in only 37 out of 17,029 incidents, or .2 percent of the time. Interestingly, asking students for an apology was used only 121 of 17,029 times, or .7 percent of the time, and behavioral contracts only 37 of 17,029, or .2 percent of the time, even though these approaches would logically appear to be easy and quite effective.

Again, findings from other studies are fairly consistent with those reported by Skiba, Peterson, and Williams. For example, after interviewing 100 middle school and 100 high school administrators representing schools of four different sizes and four different community types, James Green and Donald Barnes (1993) concluded that "actions taken in response to offenses are consistent among the four school sizes and four community types" (p. 7). The most common actions employed by administrators in their study included the following:

- Verbal reprimand
- Disciplinary notices to parents
- Conferences
- After-school detention
- Out-of-school suspension
- Expulsion

This list is quite similar to that produced by Ward Billings and John Enger (1995) as a result of their study:

- Verbal reprimand
- Detention
- In-school suspension
- Out-of-school suspension
- Expulsion

Figure 8.3

Top 10 Consequences for Referrals and Cumulative Percentages

Consequence	Percentage	Cumulative Percentage
Home Suspension	33.3	33.3
Reprimand	12.3	45.6
In-School Suspension	10.1	55.7
Parent Contact	9.4	65.1
Miscellaneous	8.6	73.7
Counseling	7.0	80.7
Conferencing	5.3	86.0
Detention	4.9	90.9
Isolation	3.7	94.6
Bus Suspension	2.2	96.8

Source: Adapted from Russell Skiba, Reece Peterson, and Tara Williams. Office referrals and suspension: Disciplinary interventions in middle schools. *Education and Treatment of Children, 20*(3), 295–315. Copyright 1997. Education and Treatment of Children.

Although the consequences for school-level misbehavior are fairly uniform, the effectiveness of these various consequences is not well studied. That is, researchers have paid little attention to the relative effectiveness of verbal reprimands versus detention and so on. However, there are some notable exceptions. "Saturday school" is one of those exceptions. John Winborn (1992) reports significant decreases in suspensions and expulsions as a result of Saturday school at the high school level. Students assigned to Saturday school spend time doing such things as writing about discipline and engaging in behavior-improvement training. Kube and Ratigan (1992) describe a Saturday program for unexcused absences. Specifically, the consequences of an unexcused absence are a class held on Saturday morning from 8:00 to 11:30, during which students must complete assignments they have missed. If students fail to complete those assignments, they must attend another Saturday class.

David Gullatt and Dwayne Lemoine (1997) report the effect of a program for truancy that might be considered particularly harsh by some because the consequences apply to parents and guardians. Gullatt and Lemoine report:

In the first three years of its implementation, over 600 cases were prosecuted resulting in 300 convictions in which a parent or guardian was fined and received some form of counseling. Since its beginning in 1989, a 45% reduction in the dropout rate has occurred at practically no cost to the school district. By keeping 800 more students on the roll, approximately $3,000 in both state and local reimbursement was received for each student based on the school district's average daily attendance. It was noted that for every 200 cases brought to court more than 400 students returned to school. (p. 7)

In summary, schools typically use a variety of consequences for violations of schoolwide rules and procedures. The following vignette depicts how a school might approach the issue of schoolwide consequences.

When students at Ames violated school rules, they were often assigned an after-school detention, which they served the day after the punishment was assigned. This plan gave students a day to inform their parents of the detention. During the detention time, students were expected to write a short description of their behavior that led to the punishment, an explanation of why the incident occurred, and their plan for avoiding the same type of incident in the future. On the surface it appeared the new detention policy was working well—until the new assistant principal began to notice that the same students were receiving detention over and over again. What was wrong? After some investigation, it became clear that students did not really mind the punishment for a number of reasons. First, the regular offenders were often not telling their parents about the detentions, skillfully crafting stories about clubs and sports events, stories that their parents apparently believed. Second, so much time passed between the infraction and the detention that students could not effectively analyze the reasons for their behavior. The written analyses were, therefore, not thoughtful or even accurate. Third, the teachers who supervised detention varied greatly in their approach, some creating an almost hostile atmosphere and others allowing students a great deal of freedom in terms of how they spent their time. The assistant principal decided it was time to revamp the policy. The changes made weren't that big, but they were significant. Parents were called immediately—by the student—when the detention was given; students wrote the analysis that night and the parents signed it. Finally, supervisory approaches became much more consistent. Predictably, many of the "regulars" in detention began to change their behavior.

ACTION STEP 4 ▼

Establish a system that allows for the early detection of students who have high potentials for violence and extreme behaviors.

The work of Tary Tobin and George Sugai (1999) has demonstrated the utility and impact of early detection of students who are at risk for future violence or extreme misbehavior. Specifically, they undertook a longitudinal study involving 526 students in which they examined the records of students in grade 6 to predict violence in grade 8. They reported the following:

> Results suggest that a discipline referral at Grade 6, for either violent or nonviolent behavior, should prompt educators and parents to intervene but with a positive behavior support plan likely to change the predicted trajectory of continual antisocial behaviors. Even a few discipline referrals in Grade 6 and, in some cases, even one referral should be recognized as a warning of more problems to come and thus a need to develop and implement preventative interventions. (p. 47)

Figure 8.4 reports the correlations between violent behavior in grade 8 and certain types of referrals in grade 6. It provides some useful behavioral categories schools might keep track of. For example, any form of violent fighting appears to be a strong indicator that future problems might appear. Additionally, harassing and nonviolent misbehavior might indicate future problems. Of course, it is important to emphasize that these types of data should not be used to typecast students. Rather, they should be used to identify students who might need extra support or help to avoid potential negative consequences of tendencies they may have. The following vignette depicts how a school might use data to help ward off problems in the future.

The counselors at Hardy Middle School spent a significant amount of their time teaching students about "bully-proofing" strategies and helping all students become aware of the dangers and consequences associated with harassment. Although

---

Figure 8.4

Correlations Between Referrals in Grade 6 and Violent Behavior in Grade 8

Type of Grade 6 Referral	Correlation
Violent Fighting	.55
Violent Harassing	.37
Nonviolent Misbehavior	.35
Out-of-School Suspension	.32

Source: Data from Tobin & Sugai (1999).

they felt their teaching was influencing students, they would probably say the most successful aspect of their program was their use of peer counselors. Eighth grade students were selected and then trained to provide support and advice to the younger students at the school. Part of their job was to talk to students who had been harassed or bullied. The other part was to work with 6th grade students who had been referred to the office for violent or harassing behavior. Although counselors always facilitated these interactions, they were almost always impressed with the way the 8th graders could connect with the young 6th grade offenders. Sometimes the 8th grade counselors had themselves been in trouble in 6th grade, which helped them to empathize with the younger students and provide sound advice and encouragement. This ongoing support often resulted in the 6th grade students not only changing their behavior but also aspiring to become peer counselors when they became 8th graders.

ACTION STEP 5 ▼

Adopt a schoolwide management program.

In previous chapters I identified programs that have specific strengths in the respective areas of rules and procedures, disciplinary interventions, teacher-student relationships, mental set, student responsibility, and beginning the school year. In describing these programs, I noted that even though they were being discussed in terms of a specific aspect of classroom management, virtually all of them addressed all or most of the critical aspects of management at least to some extent. This discussion of adopting a schoolwide program uses Think Time by Ron Nelson and Beth Carr (1999) as an example, although any of the programs described in Chapters 2 through 7 would suffice.

One important point to keep in mind when considering the adoption of a schoolwide classroom management program is that it will impose requirements on all teachers. The fact that a schoolwide program requires consistency of behavior among teachers is both the strength and the weakness of this action step. When teachers in a school exhibit consistent behavior relative to classroom management, it communicates a very powerful message to students and their parents and guardians. However, it requires that all teachers employ the behaviors dictated by the program. By definition, this decreases some of the freedom that classroom teachers typically enjoy. With this perspective in mind, consider the five major components of Think Time.

1. Catching Disruptive Behavior. When teachers observe inappropriate student behavior, the behavior is immediately noted. If the student acknowledges and stops the behavior, the class continues without further action. However, if the behavior does not stop, the teacher sends the student to the "Think Time classroom," or "TT classroom."

2. Movement to and Entering the Think Time Classroom. The manner in which students move to and enter the Think Time classroom is closely monitored. For most disruptive behaviors, a teacher asks students to go by themselves to the Think Time classroom. However, the amount of time it takes students to get to the TT classroom is tracked. If problems occur with movement to the TT Classroom, the teacher may send an escort with the disruptive student.

3. Think Time Debriefing. Debriefing on the behavior that resulted in assignment to the TT classroom is critical to the overall process. It involves the student completing a written form. The teacher in the TT classroom conducts the debriefing at his convenience. The debriefing usually involves asking students to do the following:

- Identify the behavior that was considered inappropriate.
- Identify what they need to do differently when they get back to the classroom (i.e., identify possible "replacement behaviors").
- Indicate whether they think they can perform the replacement behaviors.

With younger students it is not uncommon to use "pictorial" debriefings. That is, students are asked to draw a picture or pictures depicting their behavior, what they need to do differently to be allowed back into the regular classroom, and so on.

4. Checking the Debriefing Form. Before a student is dismissed from the TT classroom, the teacher there examines the debriefing form.

If the form has been correctly filled out, then the student can rejoin the regular classroom.

5. Rejoining the Regular Classroom. When students rejoin the regular classroom, they wait by the door. The regular classroom teacher then checks to see if the debriefing form is correct. If the student has missed work, the teacher assigns a peer to help the student catch up on that work.

Quite obviously, Think Time is a highly structured approach to management. Again, use of a schoolwide program communicates a strong sense of solidarity among school staff regarding management, but it requires teachers to agree on a set of actions and strategies that all of them will use. This requires considerable discussion and deliberation among teachers. The following vignette depicts how these deliberations might play out in a school.

"Look, one size does not fit all . . ."

"But we need a united front . . ."

"Let's remember, 'foolish consistency is the hobgoblin of little minds' and . . ."

"It takes a village . . ."

Ms. Paynter, the principal, was listening to this discussion but was becoming impatient. "Please stop with the clichés. This is getting us nowhere."

The topic was whether to adopt a schoolwide discipline program that all teachers would use in their classrooms. Ms. Paynter, at that moment, decided to take a stand—to lead: "Here is the reality. We have tried to decrease discipline problems for two years by allowing everyone to use their own individual approach. It hasn't worked. Our school has grown, and so have our problems. I have always protected your academic freedoms and have involved you in decision-making processes—and I will continue to do so. But I have to ask that you work with me

to try a more structured, consistent approach to classroom management."

Summary

Behavior management is a matter that requires consideration at the school level as well as the individual classroom level. After all, classroom management exists within the larger context of the school, and schoolwide management policies and practices set the tone for individual classroom management. Management at the school level should address the need to counteract the possible negative consequences of scheduling practices or environmental factors that might promote student misbehavior, the identification of schoolwide rules and procedures, and schoolwide consequences for violations of those rules and procedures and the design of a system that would allow for the early detection of students with tendencies for violence or extreme behavior. Adoption of a schoolwide classroom management program sends a powerful message about the importance the school attaches to this aspect of students' experience in the school.

A Final Word

This book has described various research-based approaches to classroom and school management. The basic conclusion one can infer is that every teacher and every school in the country can readily attain effective management. Decades of research provide clear guidance on the critical aspects of effective management and the strategies that work best to achieve it. Equipped with this knowledge and understanding, schools and classroom teachers can educate students in a safe, orderly, and respectful environment that maximizes the possibilities for effective teaching and real learning.

APPENDIX

A CLOSER LOOK AT RESEARCH METHODS

The concept of a meta-analysis was briefly addressed in Chapter 1. Here we consider this form of research in more depth, with particular attention to the meta-analysis that forms the basis for the recommendations in this book. (For a more technical description of the meta-analysis conducted during the development of this book, see Marzano [2003a].)

In very general terms, a meta-analysis of the research on any topic attempts to summarize the findings from the studies on that topic in quantitative terms. Typically, the findings from the studies reviewed are all translated into an *effect size*, which is defined here in the following way:

$$\frac{\text{Mean of experimental group} - \text{Mean of the control group}}{\text{The population standard deviation}}$$

By definition, this formula translates the difference between the mean of the experimental group and the mean of the control group into standard deviation units. In the context of this book, the experimental group was typically a class that employed some type of classroom management technique, and the control group was a class that did not. In Chapter 1, I described an effect size in terms of the difference in average number of disruptions between the experimental group and the control group. However, one confounding factor in terms of interpreting the findings of the meta-analysis conducted for this book is that some studies looked at one individual and others looked at whole classes. An effect size is interpreted slightly differently when a study is based on an individual as opposed to experimental and control groups. To illustrate, with single-subject designs, the misbehavior of an individual student was typically tracked before and after a particular classroom management technique was used. A technical explanation of how these pre-intervention behaviors were compared with the post-intervention behaviors to compute an effect size is described in Crosbie (1993). In general terms, one might interpret an effect size from these single-subject studies as the change in frequency of disruptions for an individual student after the classroom management technique has been used. Before the use of the classroom management technique, the student might have had some "good days" in terms of behavior (i.e., exhibited no disruptions) and some "bad days" (i.e., many disruptions). If you plotted the frequency of daily disruptions for that student over a long period of time—say, three months—you would probably obtain a distribution that approaches the normal distribution, as shown in Figure A.1.

Note that in Figure A.1 the average number of disruptions for this student on a given day is 4.0 with a standard deviation of 2.0.

However, after the use of a given classroom management technique, the distribution of disruptions for that student might resemble the left side of Figure A.2. The figure illustrates that the average number of disruptions for the student has dropped from 4.0 per day to 2.5 per day. If we assume that the standard deviation in both distributions depicted in Figure A.2 is 2.0, then we compute the effect size for the classroom management technique to be –.75 ((2.5 – 4.0)/2.0). In short, the average number of disruptions per day for that single student after the classroom management strategy has been implemented is .75 standard deviations less than the average number of disruptions per day for that student before the implementation of the classroom management technique.

In Chapter 1, I described the interpretation of an effect size in terms of the behavior

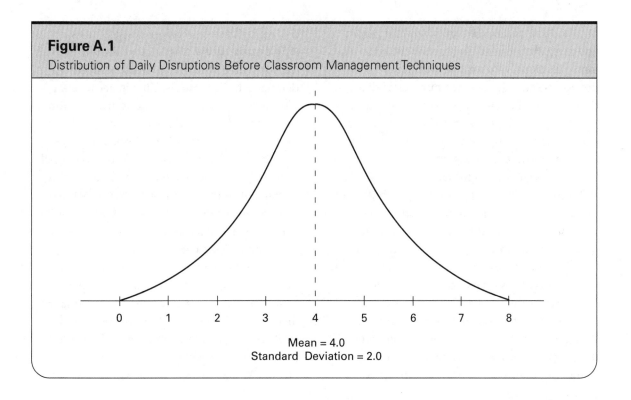

Figure A.1

Distribution of Daily Disruptions Before Classroom Management Techniques

Mean = 4.0
Standard Deviation = 2.0

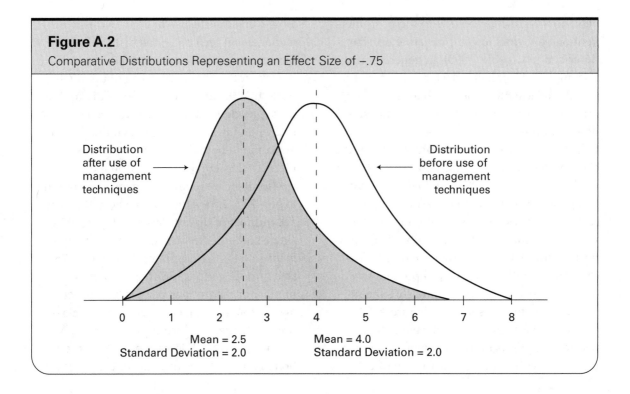

Figure A.2

Comparative Distributions Representing an Effect Size of –.75

Distribution after use of management techniques

Distribution before use of management techniques

0 1 2 3 4 5 6 7 8

Mean = 2.5
Standard Deviation = 2.0

Mean = 4.0
Standard Deviation = 2.0

of groups as opposed to an individual before and after a treatment. To contrast the two interpretations, let's assume that Figure A.1 now represents the average number of disruptions in a mathematics class. That average is 4.0 disruptions by the entire class over a single class period (as opposed to the 4.0 disruptions by a single student for an entire day.) Now let's assume that the left-hand side of Figure A.2 represents the change in the distribution of disruptions in a class that uses a specific classroom management technique. The average number of disruptions per day has dropped by .75 standard deviations. In summary, with a single-subject design, we can interpret the effect size as the decrease in the average number of disruptions for a single student. With a whole-class design, we can interpret the effect size as the decrease in the average number of disruptions for the entire class.

Regardless of whether a study uses a single-subject or a whole-class design, we can translate an effect size into a percentile decrease in disruptions. This is because an effect size is expressed in standard deviation units, and standard deviations are easily interpreted as percentiles. For example, distribution theory tells us that with normally occurring phenomena, we can expect about 34 percent of the distribution to fall between the average score and one standard deviation below the average. Thus an effect size of –1.00 for a specific management strategy means that the average number of disruptions for the experimental class is 34 percentile points less than the average number of disruptions in the class that did not use the strategy. The conversion table in Figure A.3 allows you to translate effect sizes into percentile decreases.

Figure A.3

Conversion Table for Effect Size to Percentile Decrease

Effect Size	Percentile Decrease in Disruptions	Effect Size	Percentile Decrease in Disruptions
0.00	0	−0.67	−25
−0.02	−1	−0.71	−26
−0.05	−2	−0.74	−27
−0.08	−3	−0.77	−28
−0.10	−4	−0.81	−29
−0.13	−5	−0.84	−30
−0.15	−6	−0.88	−31
−0.18	−7	−0.92	−32
−0.20	−8	−0.95	−33
−0.23	−9	−1.00	−34
−0.25	−10	−1.04	−35
−0.28	−11	−1.08	−36
−0.31	−12	−1.13	−37
−0.33	−13	−1.17	−38
−0.36	−14	−1.23	−39
−0.39	−15	−1.28	−40
−0.41	−16	−1.34	−41
−0.44	−17	−1.41	−42
−0.47	−18	−1.48	−43
−0.50	−19	−1.56	−44
−0.52	−20	−1.64	−45
−0.55	−21	−1.75	−46
−0.58	−22	−1.88	−47
−0.61	−23	−2.05	−48
−0.64	−24	−2.33	−49

As mentioned in Chapter 1, the meta-analysis conducted for this book involved more than 100 studies that produced 134 effect sizes. Figure A.4 reports the specifics of the studies used in this meta-analysis. The first column provides a number code to the studies used in the meta-analysis. These studies are listed in the References section at the end of Figure A.4. The second column, Design, identifies whether the study was based on groups or on a single subject. The third column identifies the grade level of the students involved in the study (primary, upper elementary, middle school/junior high, high school). The fourth column identifies the setting in which the study took place (regular education, self-contained classroom, resource room). Finally, the fifth column identifies the general category of classroom management for which effect sizes were computed in each study (rules and procedures, discipline, teacher-student relationship, mental set, responsibility). In most cases only one effect size was computed for each study. However, in some cases it was possible to compute more than one effect size because the study addressed multiple categories.

Figure A.4
Characteristics of Studies Used in the Meta-Analysis

Study Number	Design	Level	Class Setting	Major Category
1. Amerikaner & Summerlin (1982)	Group	Primary	Regular Education	General
2. Ayllon, Garber, & Pisor (1975)	Group	Upper Elementary	Regular Education	Discipline
3. Ayllon & Roberts (1974)	Group	Upper Elementary	Regular Education	Discipline
4. Barrish, Saunders, & Wolf (1969)	Group	Upper Elementary	Regular Education	Discipline
5. Bellaflore & Salend (1983)	Single Subject	Primary	Self-Contained	Responsibility
6. Birkimer & Brown (1979)	Group	Upper Elementary	Regular Education	Responsibility
7. Bloomquist, August, & Ostrander (1991)	Group	Upper Elementary	Regular Education	Responsibility
8. Bolstad & Johnson (1972)	Group	Primary	Regular Education	Discipline
9. Borg & Ascione (1982)	Group	Upper Elementary	Regular Education	Discipline
10. Bornstein, Hamilton, & Quevillon (1977)	Single Subject	Upper Elementary	Regular Education	Discipline
11. Broden, Hall, & Mitts (1971)	Single Subject	Middle School/ Junior High	Regular Education	Responsibility

▶ Continued...

Figure A.4
Characteristics of Studies Used in the Meta-Analysis *(continued)*

Study Number	Design	Level	Class Setting	Major Category
12. Broussard & Northup (1995)	Single Subject	Primary	Regular Education	Discipline
13. Brown, Reschly, & Sabers (1974)	Group	Primary	Regular Education	Discipline
14. Christie, Hiss, & Lozanoff (1984)	Single Subject	Upper Elementary	Regular Education	Responsibility
15. Clarke, et al. (1995)	Single Subject	Upper Elementary	Regular Education	Discipline
16. Coleman (1973)	Single Subject	Upper Elementary	Regular Education	Discipline
17. Colozzi, et al. (1986)	Single Subject	Middle School/ Junior High	Resource Room	Discipline
18. Cowen, et al. (1979)	Group	Primary	Regular Education	General
19. Crosbie (1993)	Group	Upper Elementary	Regular Education	Discipline
20. Darveaux (1984)	Single Subject	Primary	Regular Education	Discipline
21. Davis (1979)	Single Subject	Upper Elementary	Self-Contained	Responsibility
22. Deitz (1977)	Single Subject	Middle School/ Junior High	Self-Contained	Discipline
23. Deitz & Repp (1973)	Single Subject	Middle School/ Junior High	Regular Education	Discipline
24. Deitz, et al. (1978)	Single Subject	Primary	Self-Contained	Discipline
25. Dougherty & Dougherty (1977)	Group	Upper Elementary	Regular Education	Discipline
26. Doughty (1997)	Group	High School	Regular Education	Responsibility Rules/Procedures
27. Drabman & Lahey (1974)	Single Subject	Upper Elementary	Regular Education	Discipline
28. Drege & Beare (1991)	Single Subject	Primary	Self-Contained	Discipline
29. Dunlap, et al. (1995)	Single Subject	Upper Elementary	Self-Contained	Discipline
30. Dunlap, et al. (1994)	Single Subject	Upper Elementary	Self-Contained	General
31. Dunlap, et al. (1991)	Single Subject	Upper Elementary	Self-Contained	Discipline

▶ Continued...

Figure A.4
Characteristics of Studies Used in the Meta-Analysis *(continued)*

Study Number	Design	Level	Class Setting	Major Category
32. Eleftherios, Shoudt, & Strang (1972)	Group	High School	Regular Education	Discipline
33. Emmer, et al. (1982)	Group	Middle School/ Junior High	Regular Education	Discipline Rules/Procedures Mental Set
34. Emmer, et al. (1981)	Group	Upper Elementary	Regular Education	Discipline Rules/Procedures Mental Set
35. Emmer, Evertson, & Anderson (1980)	Group	Upper Elementary	Regular Education	Discipline Rules/Procedures Mental Set Relationship
36. Epstein, Repp, & Cullinan (1978)	Single Subject	Upper Elementary	Self-Contained	Discipline
37. Epstein & Goss (1978)	Single Subject	Upper Elementary	Regular Education	Discipline
38. Evans, et al. (1985)	Single Subject	Middle School/ Junior High	Regular Education	General
*39 a *39 b *39 c *39 d *39 e *39 f Evertson (1995)	Group Group Group Group Group Group	Upper Elementary Upper Elementary Upper Elementary Upper Elementary Upper Elementary High School	Regular Education Regular Education Regular Education Regular Education Regular Education Regular Education	Rules/Procedures Rules/Procedures Rules/Procedures Rules/Procedures Rules/Procedures Rules/Procedures
40. Fitzpatrick & McGreal (1983)	Group	High School	Regular Education	Rules/Procedures Discipline Relationship
41. Gottfredson, Gottfredson, & Hybl (1993)	Group	Middle School/ Junior High	Regular Education	Rules/Procedures
42. Grandy, Madsen, Jr., & De Mersseman (1973)	Group	Upper Elementary	Regular Education	Discipline
43. Grieger, Kauffman, & Grieger (1976)	Single Subject	Primary	Regular Education	Responsibility

*This report involved a number of studies from which effect sizes were computed.

▶ Continued...

Figure A.4

Characteristics of Studies Used in the Meta-Analysis *(continued)*

Study Number	Design	Level	Class Setting	Major Category
44. Guevremont & Foster (1993)	Single Subject	Upper Elementary	Regular Education	Responsibility
45. Hall, et al. (1971)	Single Subject	Middle School/ Junior High	Self-Contained	Discipline
46. Hall, Lund, & Jackson (1968)	Single Subject	Primary	Regular Education	Discipline
47. Iwata & Bailey (1974)	Single Subject	Upper Elementary	Regular Education	Discipline
48. Kent & O'Leary (1976)	Group	Upper Elementary	Regular Education	Discipline
49. Knapczyk (1988)	Single Subject	High School	Self-Contained	Discipline
50. Kubany, Weiss, & Sloggett, (1971)	Single Subject	Primary	Regular Education	Discipline
51. Lobitz (1974)	Single Subject	Upper Elementary	Regular Education	Discipline
52. Lochman (1992)	Group	Middle School/ Junior High	Regular Education	Responsibility
53. Lochman, et al. (1984)	Group	Middle School/ Junior High	Regular Education	Responsibility
54. Lochman, et al. (1985)	Group	Middle School/ Junior High	Regular Education	Responsibility
55. Lovitt, et al. (1973)	Single Subject	Upper Elementary	Self-Contained	Responsibility
56. Luiselli, et al. (1981)	Single Subject	Primary	Self-Contained	Discipline
57. Madsen, Jr., Becker, & Thomas (1968)	Single Subject	Primary	Regular Education	Discipline
58. Maglio & McLaughlin (1981)	Single Subject	High School	Regular Education	Discipline
59. Marandola & Imber (1979)	Group	Middle School/ Junior High	Self-Contained	Responsibility
60. Marholin II & Steinman (1977)	Group	Middle School/ Junior High	Regular Education	Discipline
61. McAllister, et al. (1969)	Group	High School	Regular Education	Discipline

▶ Continued...

Figure A.4

Characteristics of Studies Used in the Meta-Analysis *(continued)*

Study Number	Design	Level	Class Setting	Major Category
62. McCain & Kelley (1994)	Single Subject	Middle School/ Junior High	Regular Education	Discipline
63. Middleton & Cardedge (1995)	Single Subject	Primary	Regular Education	Responsibility
64. Mills & Bulach (1996)	Group	Middle School/ Junior High	Regular Education	Relationship
65. Nay, et al. (1976)	Group	Upper Elementary	Regular Education	Discipline
66. Nelson & Carson (1988)	Group	Upper Elementary	Regular Education	Responsibility
67. O'Leary & Becker (1967)	Group	Primary	Regular Education	Discipline
68. O'Leary & Becker (1968–1969)	Group	Upper Elementary	Regular Education	Discipline
69. O'Leary, Drabman, & Kass (1973)	Group	Upper Elementary	Regular Education	Discipline
70. Olexa & Forman (1984)	Group	Upper Elementary	Regular Education	Responsibility
71. Prinz, Blechman, & Dumas (1994)	Group	Primary	Regular Education	Discipline
72. Ramp, Ulrich, & Dulaney (1971)	Single Subject	Upper Elementary	Regular Education	Discipline
73. Repp & Karsh (1994)	Single Subject	Upper Elementary	Self-Contained	Responsibility
74. Rollins, et al. (1974)	Group	Middle School/ Junior High	Regular Education	Discipline
75. Safer, Heaton, & Parker (1981)	Group	High School	Regular Education	Discipline
76. Salend & Allen (1985)	Single Subject	Primary	Resource Room	Discipline
77. Salend & Gordon (1987)	Group	Primary	Resource Room	Discipline
78. Salend & Henry (1981)	Single Subject	Upper Elementary	Regular Education	Discipline
79. Salend, Jantzen, & Glek (1992)	Group	Primary	Self-Contained	Responsibility
80. Salend & Lamb (1986)	Group	Upper Elementary	Resource Room	Discipline
81. Salend, Whittaker, & Reeder (1992)	Group	Middle School/ Junior High	Resource Room	Responsibility

▶ Continued...

Figure A.4
Characteristics of Studies Used in the Meta-Analysis *(continued)*

Study Number	Design	Level	Class Setting	Major Category
82. Sandler, et al. (1987)	Single Subject	Upper Elementary	Self-Contained	Responsibility
83. Schilling & Cuvo (1983)	Group	High School	Self-Contained	Discipline
84. Sherrill, et al. (1996)	Group	Primary	Regular Education	Discipline
85. Simmons & Wasik (1973)	Group	Primary	Regular Education	Discipline
86. Smith, et al. (1988)	Single Subject	High School	Resource Room	Responsibility
87. Solomon & Tyne (1979)	Group	Primary	Regular Education	Discipline
88. Solomon & Wahler (1973)	Group	Middle School/ Junior High	Regular Education	Responsibility
89. Stainback, et al. (1986)	Group	Upper Elementary	Regular Education	Responsibility
90. Stern, Fowler, & Kohler (1988)	Single Subject	Middle School/ Junior High	Regular Education	Responsibility
91. Sugai & Rowe (1984)	Single Subject	High School	Resource Room	Responsibility
92. Umbreit (1995)	Single Subject	Upper Elementary	Regular Education	Discipline
93. Van Houten & Nau (1980)	Group	Upper Elementary	Self-Contained	Discipline
94. Van Houten, et al. (1982)	Single Subject	Middle School/ Junior High	Regular Education	Discipline
95. Whitman, et al. (1982)	Single Subject	Upper Elementary	Self-Contained	Responsibility
96. Wilson & Hopkins (1973)	Group	Middle School/ Junior High	Regular Education	Discipline
97. Wilson & Williams (1973)	Group	Primary	Regular Education	Discipline
98. Witt, Hannafin, & Martens (1983)	Single Subject	Upper Elementary	Regular Education	Discipline
99. Wolf, et al. (1970)	Single Subject	Upper Elementary	Regular Education	Discipline
100. Workman & Dickinson (1979)	Single Subject	Upper Elementary	Regular Education	Discipline
101. Yell (1986)	Group	Upper Elementary	Resource Room	General

References for Figure A.4

1. Amerikaner, M., & Summerlin, M. L. (1982). Group counseling with learning disabled children: Effects of social skills and relaxation training on self-concept and classroom behavior. *Journal of Learning Disabilities, 15,* 340–343.

2. Ayllon, T., Garber, S., & Pisor, K. (1975). The elimination of discipline problems through a combined school-home motivational system. *Behavior Therapy, 6,* 616–626.

3. Ayllon, T., & Roberts, M. D. (1974). Eliminating discipline problems by strengthening academic performance. *Journal of Applied Behavior Analysis, 7,* 71–76.

4. Barrish, H. H., Saunders, M., & Wolf, M. M. (1969). Good behavior game: Effects of individual contingencies for group consequences on disruptive behavior in a classroom. *Journal of Applied Behavior Analysis, 2,* 119–124.

5. Bellaflore, L. A., & Salend, S. J. (1983). Modifying inappropriate behaviors through a peer-confrontation system. *Behavioral Disorders, 8,* 274–279.

6. Birkimer, J. C., & Brown, J. H. (1979). The effects of student self-control on the reduction of children's problem behaviors. *Behavioral Disorders, 4,* 131–136.

7. Bloomquist, M. L., August, G. J., & Ostrander, R. (1991). Effects of a school-based cognitive behavioral intervention for ADHD children. *Journal of Abnormal Child Psychology, 19,* 591–605.

8. Bolstad, O. D., & Johnson, S. M. (1972). Self-regulations in the modification of disruptive classroom behavior. *Journal of Applied Behavior Analysis, 5,* 443–454.

9. Borg, W. R., & Ascione, F. R. (1982). Classroom management in mainstreaming classrooms. *Journal of Educational Psychology, 74*(1), 85–95.

10. Bornstein, P. H., Hamilton, S. B., & Quevillon, R. P. (1977). Behavior modification by long distance: Demonstration of functional control over disruptive behavior in a rural classroom setting. *Behavior Modification, 1,* 369–380.

11. Broden, M., Hall, R. V., & Mitts, B. (1971). The effect of self-recording on the classroom behavior of two eighth-grade students. *Journal of Applied Behavior Analysis, 4,* 191–199.

12. Broussard, C. D., & Northup, J. (1995). An approach to functional assessment and analysis of disruptive behavior in regular education classrooms. *School Psychology Quarterly, 10,* 151–164.

13. Brown, D., Reschly, D., & Sabers, D. (1974). Using group contingencies with punishment and positive reinforcement to modify aggressive behaviors in a Head Start classroom. *The Psychological Record, 24,* 491–496.

14. Christie, D. J., Hiss, M., & Lozanoff, B. (1984). Modification of inattentive classroom behavior. Hyperactive children's use of self-recording with teacher guidance. *Behavior Modification, 8,* 391–406.

15. Clarke, S., Dunlap, G., Foster-Johnson, L., Childs, K. E., Wilson, D., White, R., & Vera, A. (1995). Improving the conduct of students with behavioral disorders by incorporating student interests into curricular activities. *Behavioral Disorders, 20,* 221–237.

16. Coleman, R. G. (1973). A procedure for fading from experimenter-school-based to parent-home-based control of classroom behavior. *Journal of School Psychology, 11,* 71–79.

17. Colozzi, G. A., Coleman-Kennedy, M., Fay, R., Hurley, W., Magliozzi, M., Schackle, K., & Walsh, P. (1986, September). Data-based integration of a student with moderate special needs. *Education and Training of the Mentally Retarded, 21,*192–199.

18. Cowen, E. L., Orgel, A. R., Gesten, E. L., & Wilson, A. B. (1979). The evaluation of an intervention program for young schoolchildren with acting-out problems. *Journal of Abnormal Child Psychology, 7,* 381–396.

19. Crosbie, J. (1993). Interrupted time-series analysis with brief single-subject data. *Journal of Consulting and Clinical Psychology, 61,* 966–974.

20. Darveaux, D. X. (1984). The good behavior game plus merit: Controlling disruptive behavior and improving student motivation. *School Psychology Review, 13,* 510–514.

21. Davis, R. A. (1979). The impact of self-modeling on problem behaviors in school-age children. *School Psychology Digest, 8,* 128–132.

22. Deitz, S. M. (1977). An analysis of programming DRL schedules in educational settings. *Behavioral Research & Therapy, 15,* 103–111.

23. Deitz, S. M., & Repp, A. C. (1973). Decreasing classroom misbehavior through the use of DRL schedules and reinforcement. *Journal of Applied Behavior Analysis, 6,* 457–463.

24. Deitz, S. M., Slack, D. J., Schwarzmueller, E. B., Wilander, A. P., Weatherly, T. J., & Hilliard, G. (1978). Reducing inappropriate behavior in special classrooms by reinforcing average interresponse time: Interval DRL. *Behavior Therapy, 9,* 37–46.

25. Dougherty, E. H., & Dougherty, A. (1977). The daily report card: A simplified and flexible package for classroom behavior management. *Psychology in the Schools, 14,* 191–195.

26. Doughty, J. E. (1997, June). *The effect of a social skills curriculum on student performance.* Paper presented at the Annual Research Colloquium, Carrollton, GA. (ERIC Document Reproduction Service No. ED412260)

27. Drabman, R. S., & Lahey, B. B. (1974). Feedback in classroom behavior modification: Effects on the target

and her classmates. *Journal of Applied Behavior Analysis, 7*, 591–598.

28. Drege, P., & Beare, P. L. (1991). The effect of a token reinforcement system with a time-out backup consequence on the classroom behavior of E/BD students. *British Columbia Journal of Special Education, 15*, 39–46.

29. Dunlap, G., Clarke, S., Jackson, M., Wright, S., Ramos, E., & Brinson, S. (1995). Self-monitoring of classroom behaviors with students exhibiting emotional and behavioral challenges. *School Psychology Quarterly, 10*, 165–177.

30. Dunlap, G., DePerczel, M., Clarke, S., Wilson, D., Wright, S., White, R., & Gomez, A. (1994). Choice making to promote adaptive behavior for students with emotional and behavioral challenges. *Journal of Applied Behavior Analysis, 27*, 505–518.

31. Dunlap, G., Kern-Dunlap, L., Clarke, B., & Robbins, F. R. (1991). Functional assessment, curricular revision, and severe behavior problems. *Journal of Applied Behavior Analysis, 24*, 387–397.

32. Eleftherios, C. P., Shoudt, J. T., & Strang, H. R. (1972). The game machine: A technological approach to classroom control. *Journal of School Psychology, 10*, 55–60.

33. Emmer, E., Sanford, J. P., Clements, B. S., & Martin, J. (1982). *Improving classroom management and organization in junior high schools: An experimental investigation* (R&D Report No. 6153). Austin, TX: Research and Development Center for Teacher Education: The University of Texas at Austin. (ERIC Document Reproduction Service No. 261053)

34. Emmer, E., Sanford, J. P., Evertson, C. M., Clements, B. S., & Martin, J. (1981). *The classroom management improvement study: An experiment in elementary school classrooms.* Austin, TX: Research and Development Center for Teacher Education: The University of Texas at Austin. (ERIC Document Reproduction Service No. ED226452)

35. Emmer, E. T., Evertson, C. M., & Anderson, L. M. (1980). Effective classroom management at the beginning of the school year. *Elementary School Journal, 80*(5), 219–231.

36. Epstein, M. H., Repp, A. C., & Cullinan, D. (1978). Decreasing "obscure" language of behaviorally disordered children through the use of a DRL schedule. *Psychology in the Schools, 15*, 419–423.

37. Epstein, R., & Goss, C. M. (1978). Case study: A self-control procedure for the maintenance of nondisruptive behavior in an elementary school child. *Behavior Therapy, 9*, 109–117.

38. Evans, W. H., Evans, S. S., Schmid, R. E., & Pennypacker, H. S. (1985, November). The effects of exercise on selected classroom behaviors of behaviorally disordered adolescents. *Behavioral Disorders, 10*, 42–51.

39. Evertson, C. M. (1995). *Classroom organization and management program: Revalidation submission to the Program Effectiveness Panel, U.S. Department of Education.* (Tech. Report). Nashville, TN: Peabody College, Vanderbilt University. (ERIC Document Reproduction Service No. ED403247)

40. Fitzpatrick, K. A., & McGreal, T. L. (1983). The effect of training on classroom management on academic engaged time in secondary classrooms. *Illinois School Research and Development, 20*(1), 20–32.

41. Gottfredson, D. C., Gottfredson, G. D., & Hybl, L. G. (1993). Managing adolescent behavior: A multiyear, multischool study. *American Educational Research Journal, 30*, 179–215.

42. Grandy, G. S., Madsen, C. H., Jr., & De Mersseman, L. M. (1973). The effects of individual and interdependent contingencies on inappropriate classroom behavior. *Psychology in Schools, 10*, 488–493.

43. Grieger, T., Kauffman, J. M., & Grieger, R. M. (1976). Effects of peer reporting on cooperative play and aggression of kindergarten children. *Journal of School Psychology, 14*, 307–312.

44. Guevremont, D. C., & Foster, S. L. (1993). Impact of social problem-solving training on aggressive boys: Skill acquisition, behavior change, and generalization. *Journal of Abnormal Child Psychology, 21*, 13–27.

45. Hall, R. V., Fox, R., Willard, D., Goldsmith, L., Emerson, M., Owen, M., Davis, F., & Porcia, E. (1971). The teacher as observer and experimenter in the modification of disputing and talking-out behaviors. *Journal of Applied Behavior Analysis, 4*, 141–149.

46. Hall, R. V., Lund, D., & Jackson, D. (1968). Effects of teacher attention on study behavior. *Journal of Applied Behavior Analysis, 1*, 1–12.

47. Iwata, B. A., & Bailey, J. S. (1974). Reward versus cost token systems: An analysis of the effects on students and teacher. *Journal of Applied Behavior Analysis, 7*, 567–576.

48. Kent, R. N., & O'Leary, K. D. (1976). A controlled evaluation of behavior modification with conduct problem children. *Journal of Consulting and Clinical Psychology, 44*, 586–596.

49. Knapczyk, D. R. (1988). Reducing aggressive behaviors in special and regular class settings by training alternative social responses. *Behavioral Disorders, 14*, 27–39.

50. Kubany, E. S., Weiss, L. E., & Sloggett, B. B. (1971). The good behavior clock: A reinforcement/time out procedure for reducing disruptive classroom behavior. *Journal of Behavioral Therapy & Experimental Psychiatry, 2*, 173–179.

51. Lobitz, W. C. (1974). A simple stimulus cue for controlling disruptive classroom behavior. *Journal of Abnormal Child Psychology, 2*, 143–152.

52. Lochman, J. E. (1992). Cognitive-behavioral intervention with aggressive boys: Three-year follow-up and

preventive effects. *Journal of Consulting and Clinical Psychology, 60,* 426–432.

53. Lochman, J. E., Burch, P. R., Curry, J. F., & Lampron, L. B. (1984). Treatment and generalization effects of cognitive behavioral and goal setting interventions with aggressive boys. *Journal of Consulting and Clinical Psychology, 52,* 915–916.

54. Lochman, J. E., Lampron, L. B., Burch, P. R., & Curry, J. F. (1985). Client characteristics associated with behavior change for treated and untreated aggressive boys. *Journal of Abnormal Child Psychology, 13,* 527–538.

55. Lovitt, T. C., Lovitt, A. O., Eaton, M. D., & Kirkwood, M. (1973). The deceleration of inappropriate comments by a natural consequence. *Journal of School Psychology, 11,* 148–154.

56. Luiselli, J. K., Pollow, R. S., Colozzi, G. A., & Teitelbaum, M. (1981). Application of differential reinforcement to control disruptive behaviors of mentally retarded students during remedial instruction. *Journal of Mental Deficiency Research, 25,* 265–273.

57. Madsen, C. H., Jr., Becker, W. C., & Thomas, D. R. (1968). Rules, praise, and ignoring: Elements of elementary and classroom control. *Journal of Applied Behavior Analysis, 1,* 139–150.

58. Maglio, C. L., & McLaughlin, T. F. (1981). Effects of a token reinforcement system and teacher attention in reducing inappropriate verbalizations with a junior high school student. *Corrective & Social Psychiatry & Journal of Behavior Technology, Methods & Therapy, 27,* 140–145.

59. Marandola, P., & Imber, S. C. (1979). Glasser's classroom meeting: A humanistic approach to behavior change with preadolescent inner-city learning disabled children. *Journal of Learning Disabilities, 12,* 30–34.

60. Marholin, D., II, & Steinman, W. M. (1977). Stimulus control in the classroom as a function of the behavior reinforced. *Journal of Applied Behavior Analysis, 10,* 465–478.

61. McAllister, L. W., Stachowiak, J. G., Baer, D. M., & Conderman, L. (1969). The application of operant conditioning techniques in a secondary school classroom. *Journal of Applied Behavior Analysis, 2,* 277–285.

62. McCain, A. P., & Kelley, M. L. (1994). Improving classroom performance in underachieving preadolescents: The additive effects of response cost to a school-home note system. *Child & Family Behavior Therapy, 16,* 27–41.

63. Middleton, M. B., & Cardedge, G. (1995). The effects of social skills instruction and parental involvement on the aggressive behavior of African-American males. *Behavior Modification, 19,* 192–210.

64. Mills, D., & Bulach, C. (1996, March). *Behavior disordered students in collaborative/cognitive classes. Does behavior improve?* Paper presented at the National Dropout Prevention Conference, Tampa, FL. (ERIC Document Reproduction Service No. 394224)

65. Nay, W. R., Schulman, J. A., Bailey, K. G., & Huntsinger, G. M. (1976). Territory and classroom management: An exploratory case study. *Behavior Therapy, 7,* 240–246.

66. Nelson, G., & Carson, P. (1988). Evaluation of a social problem-solving skills program for third- and fourth-grade students. *American Journal of Community Psychology, 16,* 79–99.

67. O'Leary, K. D., & Becker, W. C. (1967, May). Behavior modification of an adjustment class: A token reinforcement program. *Exceptional Children, 33,* 637–642.

68. O'Leary, K. D., & Becker, W. C. (1968–69). The effects of the intensity of a teacher's reprimands on children's behavior. *Journal of School Psychology, 7,* 8–11.

69. O'Leary, K. D., Drabman, R. S., & Kass, R. E. (1973). Maintenance of appropriate behavior in a token program. *Journal of Abnormal Child Psychology, 1,* 127–138.

70. Olexa, D. F., & Forman, S. G. (1984). Effects of social problem-solving training on classroom behavior of urban disadvantaged students. *Journal of School Psychology, 22,* 165–175.

71. Prinz, R. J., Blechman, E. A., & Dumas, J. E. (1994). An evaluation of peer coping-skills training for childhood aggression. *Journal of Clinical Child Psychology, 23,* 193–203.

72. Ramp, E., Ulrich, R., Dulaney, S. (1971). Delayed timeout as a procedure for reducing disruptive classroom behavior: A case study. *Journal of Applied Behavior Analysis, 4,* 235–239.

73. Repp, A. C., & Karsh, K. G. (1994). Hypothesis-based interventions for tantrum behaviors of persons with developmental disabilities in school settings. *Journal of Applied Behavior Analysis, 27,* 21–31.

74. Rollins, H. A., McCandless, B. R., Thompson, M., & Brassell, W. R. (1974). Project success environment: An extended application of contingency management in inner-city schools. *Journal of Educational Psychology, 66,* 167–178.

75. Safer, D. J., Heaton, R. C., & Parker, F. C. (1981). A behavioral program for disruptive junior high school students: Results and follow up. *Journal of Abnormal Child Psychology, 9,* 483–494.

76. Salend, S. J., & Allen, E. M. (1985). Comparative effects of externally managed and self-managed response-cost systems on inappropriate classroom behavior. *Journal of School Psychology, 23,* 59–67.

77. Salend, S. J., & Gordon, B. D. (1987, February). A group-oriented timeout ribbon procedure. *Behavioral Disorders, 12,* 181–187.

78. Salend, S. J., & Henry, K. (1981). Response cost in mainstreamed settings. *Journal of School Psychology, 19,* 242–249.

79. Salend, S. J., Jantzen, N. R., & Glek, K. (1992). Using a peer confrontation system in a group setting. *Behavioral Disorders, 17,* 211–218.

80. Salend, S. J., & Lamb, E. A. (1986). Effectiveness of a group-managed interdependent contingency system. *Learning Disability Quarterly, 9,* 268–273.

81. Salend, S. J., Whittaker, C. R., & Reeder, E. (1992). Group evaluation: A collaborative peer-mediated behavior management system. *Exceptional Children, 59,* 203–209.

82. Sandler, A. G., Arnold, L. B., Gable, R. A., & Strain, P. S. (1987, February). Effects of peer pressure on disruptive behavior of behaviorally disordered classmates. *Behavioral Disorders, 12,* 104–111.

83. Schilling, D., & Cuvo, A. J. (1983, February). The effects of a contingency-based lottery on the behavior of a special education class. *Education and Training of the Mentally Retarded, 18,* 52–58.

84. Sherrill, J. T., O'Leary, S. G., Albertson-Kelly, J. A., & Kendziora, K. T. (1996). When reprimand consistency may or may not matter. *Behavior Modification, 20*(2), 226–236.

85. Simmons, J. T., & Wasik, B. H. (1973). Use of small group contingencies and special activity times to manage behavior in a first-grade classroom. *Journal of School Psychology, 11,* 228–238.

86. Smith, D. J., Young, K. R., West, R. P., & Rhode, G. (1988). Reducing the disruptive behavior of junior high school students: A classroom self-management procedure. *Behavioral Disorders, 13,* 231–239.

87. Solomon, R., & Tyne, T. F. (1979). A comparison of individual and group contingency systems in a first-grade class. *Psychology in the Schools, 16,* 193–200.

88. Solomon, R. W., & Wahler, R. G. (1973). Peer reinforcement control of classroom problem behavior. *Journal of Applied Behavior Analysis, 6,* 49–56.

89. Stainback, W., Stainback, S., Etscheidt, S., & Doud, J. (1986, Fall). A nonintrusive intervention for acting out behavior. *Teaching Exceptional Children, 18,* 38–41.

90. Stern, G. W., Fowler, S. A., & Kohler, F. W. (1988). A comparison of two intervention roles: Peer monitor and point earner. *Journal of Applied Behavior Analysis, 21,* 103–109.

91. Sugai, G., & Rowe, P. (1984, February). The effect of self-recording on out-of-seat behavior of an EMR student. *Education and Training of the Mentally Retarded, 19,* 23–28.

92. Umbreit, J. (1995). Functional assessment and intervention in a regular classroom setting for the disruptive behavior of a student with attention deficit hyperactivity disorder. *Behavioral Disorders, 20,* 267–278.

93. Van Houten, R. V., & Nau, P. A. (1980). A comparison of the effects of fixed and variable ratio schedules of reinforcement on the behavior of deaf children. *Journal of Applied Behavior Analysis, 13,* 13–21.

94. Van Houten, R. V., Nau, P. A., MacKenzie-Keating, S. E., Sameoto, D., & Colavecchia, B. (1982). An analysis of some variables influencing the effectiveness of reprimands. *Journal of Applied Behavior Analysis, 15,* 65–83.

95. Whitman, T. L., Scibak, J. W., Butler, K. M., Richter, R., & Johnson, M. R. (1982). Improving classroom behavior in mentally retarded children through correspondence training. *Journal of Applied Behavior Analysis, 15,* 545–564.

96. Wilson, C. W., & Hopkins, B. L. (1973). The effects of contingent music on the intensity of noise in junior high home economics classes. *Journal of Applied Behavior Analysis, 6,* 269–275.

97. Wilson, S. H., & Williams, R. L. (1973). The effects of group contingencies on first graders' academic and social behaviors. *Journal of School Psychology, 11,* 110–117.

98. Witt, J. C., Hannafin, M. J., & Martens, B. K. (1983). Home based reinforcement: Behavioral covariation between academic performance and inappropriate behavior. *Journal of School Psychology, 21,* 337–348.

99. Wolf, M. M., Hanley, E. L., King, L. A., Lachowicz, J., & Giles, D. K. (1970, October). The timer game: A variable interval contingency for the management of out-of-seat behavior. *Exceptional Children, 37,* 67–73.

100. Workman, E. A., & Dickinson, D. J. (1979). The use of covert positive reinforcement in the treatment of a hyperactive child: An empirical case study. *Journal of School Psychology, 17,* 67–73.

101. Yell, M. L. (1986). The effects of jogging on the rates of selected target behaviors of behaviorally disordered students. *Behavioral Disorders, 13,* 273–279.

REFERENCES

Adelman, H. S., & Taylor, L. (2002). School counselors and school reform: New directions. *Professional School Counselors, 5*(4), 235–248.

American Psychiatric Association. (2000). *Diagnostic and statistical manual of mental disorders* (text revision). Washington, DC: Author.

Anderson, J. R. (1983). *The architecture of cognition.* Cambridge, MA: Harvard University Press.

Anderson, J. R. (1995). *Learning and memory: An integrated approach.* New York: John Wiley & Sons.

Anderson, J. R., Reder, L. M., & Simon, H. A. (1995). *Applications and misapplications of cognitive psychology to mathematics education.* Unpublished paper, Carnegie Mellon University, Department of Psychology, Pittsburgh, PA. Available: http://act.psy.cmu.edu/personal/ja/misapplied.html

Anderson, J. R., Reder, L. M., & Simon, H. A. (1996). Situated learning and education. *Educational Researcher, 25*(4), 5–11.

Anderson, L., Evertson, C., & Emmer, E. (1980). Dimensions in classroom management derived from recent research. *Journal of Curriculum Studies, 12,* 343–356.

Barr, A. S. (1958). Characteristics of successful teachers. *Phi Delta Kappan, 39,* 282–284.

Barr, R. D., & Parrett, W. H. (1995). *Hope at last for at-risk youth.* Boston: Allyn & Bacon.

Battistich, V., Watson, M., Solomon, D., Schaps, E., & Solomon, J. (1991). The child development project: A comprehensive program for the development of prosocial character. In W. M. Kurtines & J. L. Gewirtz (Eds.), *Handbook of moral behavior and development: Vol. 3. Application* (pp. 1–34). Hillsdale, NJ: Erlbaum.

Bear, G. G. (1998). School discipline in the United States: Prevention, control, and long-term social development. *School Psychology Review, 27*(1), 14–32.

Berliner, D. C. (1986). In pursuit of the expert pedagogue. *Educational Researcher, 15*(7), 5–13.

Billings, W. H., & Enger, J. M. (1995, November 8–10). *Perceptions of Missouri high school principals regarding the effectiveness of in-school suspension as a disciplinary procedure.* Paper presented at the annual meeting of the Midsouth Educational Research Association, Biloxi, MS. (ERIC Document Reproduction No. ED392169)

Bishop, G. G. (1989). Evaluation of the Boy's Town Motivation System in a public school setting. *Dissertation Abstracts International, 50*(12), 5837B.

Blatt, S. J. (1995). The destructiveness of perfectionism: Implications for the treatment of depression. *American Psychologist, 50*(12), 1003–1020.

Borg, W. R., & Ascione, F. A. (1982). Classroom management in elementary mainstreaming classrooms. *Journal of Educational Psychology, 74*(1), 85–95.

Brekelmans, M., Wubbels, T., & Creton, H. A. (1990). A study of student perceptions of physics teacher behavior. *Journal of Research in Science Teaching, 27,* 335, 350.

Brickman, J. B. (1995). The effects of a preventive social skills training program on the social skills, self-concept, peer acceptance and academic achievement of early adolescents. *Dissertation Abstracts International, 56*(3), 865A.

Brophy, J. E. (1996). *Teaching problem students.* New York: Guilford.

Brophy, J. E., & Evertson, C. M. (1976). *Learning from teaching: A developmental perspective.* Boston, MA: Allyn & Bacon.

Brophy, J. E., & McCaslin, N. (1992). Teachers' reports of how they perceive and cope with problem students. *Elementary School Journal, 93,* 3–68.

Buckley, P. K., & Cooper, J. M. (1978, April). *An ethnographic study of an elementary school teacher's establishment and maintenance of group norms.* Paper presented at the annual meeting of the American Educational Research Association, Toronto, Canada.

Caffyn, R. E. (1989). Attitudes of British secondary school teachers and pupils to rewards and punishments. *Educational Research, 31,* 210–220.

Cahen, S., & Davis, D. (1987). A between–grade levels approach to the investigation of the absolute effects of schooling on achievement. *American Educational Research Journal, 24,* 1–2.

Cain, A. F. H. (1990). Social skills training (acceptance, learning disabled, emotionally handicapped). *Dissertation Abstracts International, 52*(3), 877–878A.

Callahan, C. M., & Rivera, F. P. (1992). Urban high school youth and handguns: A school-based survey. *Journal of the American Medical Association, 206,* 3038–3042.

Camp, B. W., & Bash, M. S. (1985a). *Think aloud: Increasing social and cognitive skills—A problem-solving program for children. Classroom program grades 1–2.* Champaign, IL: Research Press.

Camp, B. W., & Bash, M. S. (1985b). *Think aloud: Increasing social and cognitive skills—A problem-solving program for children. Classroom program grades 3–4.* Champaign, IL: Research Press.

Camp, B. W., & Bash, M. S. (1985c). *Think aloud: Increasing social and cognitive skills—A problem-solving program for children. Classroom program grades 5–6.* Champaign, IL: Research Press.

Canter, L., & Canter, M. (1976). *Assertive discipline: A take-charge approach for today's educators.* Seal Beach, CA: Canter & Associates.

Canter, L., & Canter, M. (1992). *Assertive discipline: Positive behavior management for today's classroom.* Santa Monica, CA: Canter & Associates.

Carnine, D., & Kameenui, E. J. (Eds.). (1992). *Higher order thinking: Designing curriculum for mainstream students.* Austin, TX: Pro-ed.

Carr, E. G., & Durand, V. M. (1985). Reducing behavior problems through functional communication training. *Journal of Applied Behavior Analysis, 18,* 111–126.

Cartledge, G., & Milburn, J. F. (1978). The case for teaching social skills in the classroom: A review. *Review of Educational Research, 48*(1), 133–156.

Centers for Disease Control and Prevention (2002). *CDC study confirms ADHD/learning disability link.* Retrieved May 4, 2002, from the World Wide Web http://www.medscape.com/viewarticle/434240.

Charles, C. M. (1996). *Building classroom discipline* (5th ed.). White Plains, NY: Longman.

Charlop, M. H., Burgio, L. D., Iwata, B. A., & Ivancic, M. T. (1988). Stimulus variation as a means of enhancing punishment effects. *Journal of Applied Behavior Analysis, 21,* 89–93.

Chiu, L. H., & Tulley, M. (1997). Student preferences of teacher discipline styles. *Journal of Instructional Psychology, 24*(3), 168–175.

Christenson, S. L., Rounds, T., & Gorney, D. (1992). Family factors and student achievement: An avenue to increase students' success. *School Psychology Quarterly, 7*(3), 178–206.

Ciechalski, J. C., & Schmidt, M. W. (1995). The effects of social skills training on students with exceptionalities. *Elementary School Guidance and Counseling, 29*(3), 217–222.

Coldron, J., & Boulton, P. (1996). What do parents mean when they talk about discipline in relation to their children's school? *British Journal of Sociology of Education, 17*(1), 53–64.

Combs, A. W. (1982). *A personal approach to teaching: Beliefs that make a difference.* Boston: Allyn & Bacon.

Committee for Children. (1991). *The second step violence prevention curriculum.* Seattle, WA: Author.

Cotton, K. (1990). *School improvement series. Close-up #9: Schoolwide and classroom discipline.* Portland, OR: Northwest Regional Educational Laboratory.

Crago, M., Shisslak, C. M., & Estes, L. S. (1996). Eating disturbances among minority groups: A review. *International Journal of Eating Disorders, 19,* 239–248.

Crespi, T. D. (2001, December). Number of homeless children in U.S. rising. *Counseling Today, 44*(6), 7.

Crosbie, J. (1993). Interrupted time-series analysis with brief single-subject data. *Journal of Consulting and Clinical Psychology, 61,* 966–974.

Crosscope-Happel, C., Hutchins, D. E., Getz, H. G., Hayes, G. L. (2000). Male anorexia nervosa: A new focus. *Journal of Mental Health Counseling, 22*(4), 365–370.

Curwin, R. L., & Mendler, A. N. (1988). *Discipline with dignity.* Alexandria, VA: Association for Supervision and Curriculum Development.

Deitz, S. M., & Repp, A. C. (1973). Decreasing classroom misbehavior through the use of DRL schedules and reinforcement. *Journal of Applied Behavior Analysis, 6,* 457–463.

Dougherty, K. C. (1989). Effects of a social skills training program on the academic performance of underachieving adolescents. *Dissertation Abstracts International, 50*(6), 1600A.

Doughty, J. E. (1997, June). *The effect of a social skills curriculum on student performance.* Paper presented at the Annual Research Colloquium, Carrollton, GA. (ERIC Document Reproduction Service No. ED412260)

Doyle, W. (1986). Classroom organization and management. In M. C. Wittrock (Ed.), *Handbook of research on teaching* (3rd ed., pp. 392–431). New York: Macmillan.

Doyle, W. (1990). Classroom management techniques. In O. C. Moles (Ed.), *Student discipline strategies: Research and practice* (pp. 113–129). Albany, NY: State University of New York Press.

Drabman, R., & Spitalnik, R. (1973). Social isolation as a punishment procedure: A controlled study. *Journal of Experimental Child Psychology, 5,* 236–249.

Dreikurs, R. (1968). *Psychology in the classroom* (2nd ed.). New York: Harper & Row.

Dreikurs, R., Grunwald, B., & Pepper, F. (1982). *Maintaining sanity in the classroom: Classroom management techniques* (2nd ed.). New York: Harper & Row.

Dunn, N. A., & Baker, S. B. (2002). Readiness to serve students with disabilities: A survey of elementary school counselors. *Professional School Counselors, 5*(4), 277–284.

Eisenhart, M. (1977, May). *Maintaining control: Teacher competence in the classroom.* Paper presented at the American Anthropological Association, Houston, TX.

Elam, S. M., Rose, L. C., & Gallup, A. M. (1996, September). The 28th annual Phi Delta Kappa/Gallup poll of the public's attitudes toward the public schools. *Phi Delta Kappan,* 41–58.

Ellis, A. (1977). The basic clinical theory of rational-emotive therapy. In A. Ellis & R. Grieger (Eds.), *Handbook of rationale-emotive therapy.* New York: Springer.

Emmer, E. T. (1984). *Classroom management: Research and implications.* (R & D Report No. 6178). Austin, TX: Research and Development Center for Teacher Education, University of Texas. (ERIC Document Reproduction Service No. ED251448)

Emmer, E. T., Evertson, C., & Anderson, L. (1980). Effective classroom management at the beginning of the school year. *Elementary School Journal, 80*(5), 219–231.

Emmer, E. T., Evertson, C. M., & Worsham, M. E. (2003). *Classroom management for secondary teachers* (6th ed.). Boston: Allyn & Bacon.

Emmer, E. T., Sanford, J. P., Clements, B. S., & Martin, J. (1982). *Improving classroom management and organization in junior high schools: An experimental investigation.* Austin, TX: Research and Development Center for Teacher Education, University of Texas. (R & D Report No. 6153). (ERIC Document Reproduction Service No. ED261053)

Emmer, E. T., Sanford, J. P., Evertson, C. M., Clements, B. S., & Martin, J. (1981). *The classroom management improvement study: An experiment in elementary school classrooms.* Austin, TX: Research and Development Center for Teacher Education, University of Texas. (R & D Report No. 6050). (ERIC Document Reproduction Service No. ED226452)

Erk, R. R. (2000). Five frameworks for increasing understanding and effective treatment for attention-deficit/hyperactivity disorder: Predominately inattentive type. *Journal of Counseling and Development 78*(4), 389–399.

Evertson, C. M. (1995). *Classroom organization and management program: Revalidation submission to the Program Effectiveness Panel, U.S. Department of Education.* (Tech. Report). Nashville, TN: Peabody College, Vanderbilt University. (ERIC Document Reproduction Service No. ED403247)

Evertson, C. M., & Emmer, E. T. (1982). Preventive classroom management. In D. Duke (Ed.), *Helping teachers manage classrooms* (pp. 2–31). Alexandria, VA: Association for Supervision and Curriculum Development.

Evertson, C. M., Emmer, E. T., Sanford, J. P., & Clements, B. S. (1983). Improving classroom management: An experiment in elementary classrooms. *Elementary School Journal, 84*(2), 173–188.

Evertson, C. M., Emmer, E. T., & Worsham, M. E. (2003). *Classroom management for elementary teachers* (6th ed.). Boston: Allyn and Bacon.

Evertson, C. M., & Harris, A. (1999). Support for managing learning-centered classrooms: The classroom organization and management program. In H. J. Freiberg (Ed.), *Beyond behaviorism: Changing the classroom management paradigm* (pp. 59–74). Boston: Allyn & Bacon.

Fahringer, M. (1996). The effects of social skills training on the writing skills of middle school students with learning disabilities. *Dissertation Abstracts International, 57*(4), 1559A.

Fan, X., & Chen, M. (2001). Parental involvement and students' academic achievement: A meta-analysis. *Educational Psychology Review, 13*(1), 1–22.

Foxx, R. M. (1978). An overview of overcorrection. *Journal of Pediatric Psychology, 3*, 97–101.

Freeman, B. (1994). Power motivation and youth: An analysis of troubled students and student leaders. *Journal of Counseling and Development, 72*(6), 661–671.

Fry, P., & Gabriel, H. (1994). Preface: The cultural construction of gender and aggression. *Sex Roles, 30*, 165–167.

Furlong, M. J., Morrison, G. M., & Dear, J. D. (1994). Addressing school violence as part of schools' educational mission. *Preventing School Failure, 38*(3), 10–17.

Furst, D. W., Terracina, C., Criste, A., Dowd, T., & Daly, D. L. (1995). *Reducing violent and disruptive behavior in elementary schools.* Poster session accepted for presentation at the 1995 Annual American Psychological Association Convention, New York.

Gathercoal, P. (1993). *Judicious discipline* (3rd ed.). San Francisco: Caddo Gap Press.

Glass, G. V. (1976). Primary, secondary, and meta-analysis of research. *Educational Researcher, 5*, 3–8.

Glass, G. V., McGaw, B., & Smith, M. L. (1981). *Meta-analysis in social research.* Beverly Hills, CA: Sage Publications.

Glasser, W. (1969). *Schools without failure.* New York: Harper & Row.

Glasser, W. (1986). *Control theory in the classroom.* New York: Harper & Row.

Glasser, W. (1990). *The quality school: Managing students without coercion.* New York: Harper & Row.

Goldstein, A. P., & Pentz, M. A. (1984). Psychological skill training and the aggressive adolescent. *School Psychology Review, 13*, 311–323.

Goldstein, A. P., Sprafkin, R. P., Gershaw, N. J., & Klein, P. (1980). *Skillstreaming the adolescent: A structured learning approach to teaching prosocial skills.* Champaign, IL: Research Press.

Good, T. L. (1982). How teachers' expectations affect results. *American Education, 18*(10), 25–32.

Good, T. L., & Brophy, J. E. (1994). *Looking in classrooms* (6th ed.). New York: Harper Collins.

Good, T. L., & Brophy, J. E. (1995). *Contemporary educational psychology* (5th ed.). White Plains, NY: Longman.

Good, T. L., & Brophy, J. E. (2003). *Looking in classrooms* (9th ed.). Boston: Allyn & Bacon.

Gottfredson, D. C., Marciniak, E. M., Birdseye, A. T., & Gottfredson, G. D. (1995). Increasing teacher expectations for student achievement. *Journal of Educational Research, 88*(3), 155–163.

Grayson, D. A., & Martin, M. D. (1985). *Gender expectations and student achievement: Participant manual.* Downey, CA: Los Angeles County Office of Education.

Green, J., & Barnes, D. (1993). *Discipline in secondary schools: How administrators deal with student misconduct.* Muncie, IN: Teachers College, Ball State University. (ERIC Document Reproduction Service No. ED357507)

Green, K. D., Forehand, R., Beck, S. J., & Vosk, B. (1980). An assessment of the relationship among measures of children's social competence and children's academic achievement. *Child Development, 51*(4), 1149–1156.

Grogger, J. (1997). Local violence and educational attainment. *The Journal of Human Resources, 32*(4), 659–682.

Gullat, D. E. & Lemoine, A. A. (1997). Truancy: What's a principal to do? *American Secondary Education, 16*(1), 7–12.

Harris, K. R. (1985). Definitional, parametric, and procedural considerations in timeout interventions and research. *Exceptional Children, 51*, 279–288.

Harrop, A., & Williams, T. (1992). Rewards and punishments in the primary school: Pupils' perceptions and teachers' usage. *Educational Psychology in Practice, 7*, 211–215.

Hart, V. H. (1996). Effects of social skills training and cross-age tutoring on academic achievement and social behaviors of girls with learning disabilities. *Dissertation Abstracts International, 57*(5), 1960A.

Harvard Medical Newsletter. (2000). *Gay youth at risk, 16*(9), 7.

Hattie, J. A. (1992). Measuring the effects of schooling. *Australian Journal of Education, 36*(1), 5–13.

Haycock, K. (1998). Good teaching matters . . . a lot. *Thinking K–16, 3*(2), 1–14.

Herr, E. L. (2002). School reform and perspectives on the role of school counselors: A century of proposals for change. *Professional School Counseling 5*(4), 220–234.

Houghton, S., Merrett, F., & Wheldall, F. (1988). The attitudes of British secondary school pupils to praise, rewards, punishments and reprimands. *New Zealand Journal of Educational Psychology, 23*, 203–214.

Hunt, M. (1997). *How science takes stock: The story of meta-analysis.* New York: Russell Sage Foundation.

Hunter, M. (1969). *Teach more—faster!* El Segundo, CA: TIP Publications.

Irvin, L. K., & Lundervold, D. A. (1988). Social validation of decelerative (punishment) procedures by special educators of severely handicapped students. *Research in Developmental Disabilities, 9*, 331–350.

Johnson, D. W., & Johnson, R. T. (1999). *Learning together and alone: Cooperative, competitive, and individualistic learning* (5th ed.). Boston: Allyn & Bacon.

Johnson, P. (2001). Dimensions of functioning in alcoholic and nonalcoholic families. *Journal of Mental Health, 23*(2), 127–136.

Joyce, B., & Showers, B. (1988). *Student achievement through staff development.* White Plains, NY: Longman.

Kaufman, K. F., & O'Leary, K. D. (1972). Reward, cost, and self-evaluation procedures for disruptive adolescents in a psychiatric hospital at school. *Journal of Applied Behavior Analysis, 5,* 293–309.

Kaufman, L. H. (1995). The effects of attentional and social skills training on academic achievement. *Dissertation Abstracts International, 56*(9), 5173B.

Kearney, P., Plax, T. G., Hays, E. R., & Ivey, M. J. (1991). College teacher misbehaviors: What students don't like about what teachers say and do. *Communication Quarterly, 39*(4), 309–324.

Kelly, C. R. (1997). *Improving student discipline at the primary level.* Master's Action Research Project, Saint Xavier University and IRI Skylight Field-Based Master's Program. (ERIC Document Reproduction Service No. ED412007)

Kerman, S., Kimball, T., & Martin, M. (1980). *Teacher expectations and student achievement.* Bloomington, IN: Phi Delta Kappan.

Kingery, P. M., McCoy-Simandle, L., & Clayton, R. (1997). Risk factors for adolescent violence: The importance of vulnerability. *School Psychology International, 18,* 49–60.

Kleiner, C. (2002, April 29). Breaking the cycle: Can children of convicts learn not to be like their parents? *U.S. News and World Report.* Retrieved December 7, 2002, from http:\\www.usnews.com.

Kohn, A. (1993). *Punished by rewards: The trouble with gold stars, incentive plans, A's, praise and other bribes.* Boston: Houghton Mifflin.

Kohn, A. (1996). *Beyond discipline: From compliance to community.* Alexandria, VA: Association for Supervision and Curriculum Development.

Kounin, J. S. (1970). *Discipline and group management in classrooms.* New York: Holt, Rinehart & Winston.

Kounin, J. S. (1983). *Classrooms: Individual or behavior settings? Micrographs in teaching and learning.* (General Series No. 1). Bloomington, IN: Indiana University, School of Education. (ERIC Document Reproduction Service No. 240070)

Kube, B., & Ratigan, G. (1992). Putting the attendance policy to the test. *The Clearing House, 65*(3), 348–350.

Langer, E. J. (1989). *Mindfulness.* Reading, MA: Addison-Wesley.

Langer, E. J., & Rodin, J. (1976). The effects of enhanced personal responsibility for the aged. *Journal of Personality and Social Psychology, 34,* 191–198.

Langer, E. J., & Weinman, C. (1981). When thinking disrupts intellectual performance: Mindlessness in an overlearned task. *Personality and Social Psychology Bulletin, 7,* 240–243.

Larson, J. (1998). Managing student aggression in high schools: Implications for practice. *Psychology in the Schools, 35*(3), 283–295.

Larson, K. A. (1989). Task-related and interpersonal problem-solving training for increasing school success in high-risk young adolescents. *Remedial and Special Education, 10*(5), 32–42.

Leal, R. (1994). Conflicting views of discipline in San Antonio schools. *Education and Urban Society, 27*(1), 35–44.

Leary, T. (1957). *An interpersonal diagnosis of personality.* New York: Ronald Press Company.

Lindsay, P. H., & Norman, D. A. (1977). *Human information processing.* New York: Academic Press.

Litow, L., & Pumroy, D. K. (1975). A brief review of classroom group-oriented contingencies. *Journal of Applied Behavior Analysis, 8,* 341–347.

Lobitz, W. C. (1974). A simple stimulus cue for controlling disruptive classroom behavior. *Journal of Abnormal Child Psychology, 2,* 143–152.

Long, J. D., & Frye, V. H. (1985). *Making it till Friday: A guide to successful classroom management* (3rd ed.). Princeton, NJ: Princeton Book Co.

Lowry, R., Sleet, D., Duncan, C., Powell, K., & Kolbe, L. (1995). Adolescents at risk for violence. *Educational Psychology Review, 7*(1), 7–39.

Luongo, P. F. (2000). Partnering child welfare, juvenile justice, and behavioral health with schools. *Professional School Counseling, 3*(5), 308–314.

Madsen, C. H., Jr., Becker, W. C., & Thomas, D. R. (1968). Rules, praise, and ignoring: Elements of elementary classroom control. *Journal of Applied Behavior Analysis, 1,* 139–150.

Martini, M. (1995). Features of home environments associated with school success. *Early Child Development and Care, 3,* 49–68.

Marzano, R. J. (2000a). *A new era of school reform: Going where the research takes us.* Aurora, CO: Mid-continent Research for Education and Learning. (ERIC Document Reproduction Service No. ED454255)

Marzano, R. J. (2000b). *Transforming classroom grading.* Alexandria, VA: Association for Supervision and Curriculum Development.

Marzano, R. J. (2003a). *A quantitative synthesis of research on classroom management.* Paper submitted for publication.

Marzano, R. J. (2003b). *What works in schools: Translating research into action.* Alexandria, VA: Association for Supervision and Curriculum Development.

Marzano, R. J., Pickering, D. J., Arredondo, D. E., Blackburn, G. J., Brandt, R. S., Moffett, C. A., Paynter, D. E., Pollock, J. E., & Whisler, J. S. (1997). *Dimensions of learning:*

Teacher's manual (2nd ed.). Alexandria, VA: Association for Supervision and Curriculum Development.

Marzano, R. J., Pickering, D. J., & McTighe, J. (1993). *Assessing student outcomes: Performance assessment using the Dimensions of Learning Model.* Alexandria, VA: Association for Supervision and Curriculum Development.

Marzano, R. J., Pickering, D. J., & Pollock, J. E. (2001). *Classroom instruction that works: Research-based strategies for increasing student achievement.* Alexandria, VA: Association for Supervision and Curriculum Development.

McCombs, B. L., & Whisler, J. S. (1997). *The learner-centered classroom and school.* San Francisco: Jossey-Bass.

McEwan, B., Gathercoal, P., & Nimmo, V. (March, 1997). *An examination of the application of constitutional concepts as an approach to classroom management: Four studies of judicious discipline in varied classroom settings.* Paper presented at the annual meeting of the American Educational Research Association, Chicago. (ERIC Document Reproduction Service No. ED418031)

McFadden, A. C., Marsch, G. E., Price, B. J., & Hwang, Y. (1992). A study of race and gender bias in the punishment of school children. *Education and Treatment of Children, 15,* 140–146.

McGinnis, E., & Goldstein, A. P. (1984). *Skillstreaming the elementary school child: A guide for teaching prosocial skills.* Champaign, IL: Research Press.

McGinnis, E., & Goldstein, A. P. (1990). *Skillstreaming in early childhood: Teaching prosocial skills to the preschool and kindergarten child.* Champaign, IL: Research Press.

Meadows, N., Neel, R. S., Parker, G., & Timo, K. (1991). A validation of social skills for students with behavioral disorders. *Behavioral Disorders, 16*(3), 200–210.

Meichenbaum, D. (1977). *Cognitive-behavior modification.* New York: Plenum Press.

Merrett, F., & Tang, W. M. (1994). The attitudes of British primary school pupils to praise, rewards, punishments and reprimands. *British Journal of Educational Psychology, 64,* 91–103.

Miller, A. M., Ferguson, E., & Simpson, R. (1998). The perceived effectiveness of rewards and sanctions in primary schools: Adding in the parental perspective. *Educational Psychology, 18*(1), 55–64.

Miller, L. (1994, September 7). Violence, discipline, top public's school concerns, poll finds. *Education Week,* p. 7.

Moskowitz, G., & Hayman, J. (1976). Success strategies of inner-city teachers: A year-long study. *Journal of Educational Research, 69,* 283–289.

Narayan, J. S., Heward, W. L., Gardner, R., Courson, F. H., & Omness, C. K. (1990). Using response cards to increase student participation in an elementary classroom. *Journal of Applied Behavior Analysis, 21,* 483–490.

Nastasi, B. K., & Clements, D. H. (1991). Research on cooperative learning: Implications for practice. *School Psychology Review, 20,* 110–131.

National Education Goals Panel. (1994, August). *Data volume for the national education goals report, Vol. 1: National data.* Washington, DC: Author.

Nelson, J. R., Martella, R., & Galand, B. (1998). The effects of teaching school expectations and establishing a consistent consequence on formal office disciplinary actions. *Journal of Emotional and Behavioral Disorders, 4*(3), 153–161.

Nelson, R., & Carr, B. A. (1999). *Think time strategy for schools: Bringing order to the classroom* (2nd ed.). Longmont, CO: Sopris West.

Netolicky, C. (1998). *Strike four: An educational paradigm servicing troublesome behavior students.* Perth, Australia: Edith Cowan University. (ERIC Document Reproduction Service No. ED420004)

Noguera, P. A. (1995). Preventing and producing violence: A critical analysis of responses to school violence. *Harvard Educational Review, 65*(2), 189–212.

Nowicki, S., & Duke, M. (1992). *Helping the child who doesn't fit in.* Atlanta, GA: Peachtree.

O'Brien, K. (1998). *Frequency of teacher intervention in hallway misconduct.* (EDIS 7788, Field Project). Charlottesville, VA: University of Virginia. (ERIC Document Reproduction Service No. ED421793)

O'Leary, K. D., Becker, W. C., Evans, M. B., & Saudargas, R. A. (1969). A token reinforcement program in a public school: A replication and systematic analysis. *Journal of Applied Behavior Analysis, 2,* 3–13.

Pinker, S. (1994). *The language instinct: How the mind creates language.* New York: Harper Perennial.

Plax, T. G., & Kearney, P. (1990). Classroom management: Structuring the classroom for work. In J. Daly, G. Friedrich, & A. Vangelesti (Eds.), *Teaching communication: Theory, research, and methods* (pp. 223–236). Hillsdale, NJ: Erlbaum.

Porter, G., Epp, L., & Bryant, S. (2000). Collaboration among school mental health professionals: A necessity not a luxury. *Professional School Counseling, 3*(5), 315–322.

Reitz, A. L. (1994). Implementing comprehensive classroom-based programs for students with emotional and behavioral problems. *Education and Treatment of Children, 17,* 312–331.

Rembolt, C., & Zimman, R. N. (1996). *Respect and protect: A practical, step-by-step violence prevention and intervention program for schools and communities.* Minneapolis, MN: Johnson Institute-QVS.

Rhode, G., Morgan, D. P., & Young, K. R. (1983). Generalization and maintenance of treatment gains of behaviorally handicapped students from resource rooms to regular classrooms using self-evaluation procedures. *Journal of Applied Behavior Analysis, 16,* 171–188.

Robinson, R. L. (1985). Investigation of three specific intervention strategies to reduce the attrition rate of potential high school dropouts. (Volumes I and II: Group guidance, social skills, tutoring, achievement motivation). *Dissertation Abstracts International, 47*(6), 2029A.

Rosenshine, B. (1983). Teaching functions in instructional programs. *Elementary School Journal, 83*(4), 335–351.

Rosenthal, R., & Jacobson, L. (1968). *Pygmalion in the classroom: Teacher expectation and pupils' intellectual development.* New York: Holt, Rinehart & Winston.

Ross, C. (2002). *Quoted as Chief Executive Director of Children and Adults with Attention Deficit/Hyperactivity Disorder (CHADD).* Retrieved July 18, 2002, from the World Wide Web http//www.medscape.com/viewarticle/434240.

Sadker, M., & Sadker, D. (1994). *Failing at fairness: How America's schools cheat girls.* New York: Macmillan.

Sanders, W. L., & Horn, S. P. (1994). The Tennessee value-added assessment system (TVAAS): Mixed-model methodology in educational assessment. *Journal of Personnel Evaluation in Education, 8,* 299–311.

Sanford, J. P., & Evertson, C. M. (1981). Classroom management in a low SES junior high: Three case studies. *Journal of Teacher Education, 32*(1), 34–38.

Sanson, A., Prior, M., Smart, D., & Oberklaid, F. (1993). Gender differences in aggression in childhood: Implications for a peaceful world. *Australian Psychologist, 28,* 86–92.

Sewall, A. M., & Chamberlin, G. D. (1997). *Safety or discipline: The real issue in public schools.* Unpublished paper, University of Arkansas at Little Rock. (ERIC Document Reproduction Service No. ED417470)

Shaffer, D., Gould, M. S., Fisher, P., Trautment, P., Moreau, D., Kleinmann, M., & Flory, M. (1998). Psychiatric diagnosis in child and adolescent suicide. *Archives of General Psychiatry, 53,* 339–348.

Shapiro, E. S., & Cole, C. L. (1994). *Behavior change in the classroom: Self-management interventions.* New York: Guilford Press.

Sharpe, P., Wheldall, K., & Merrett, F. (1987). The attitudes of British secondary school pupils to praise and rewards. *Educational Studies, 13,* 293–302.

Sheets, R. (1994, February). *Student voice: Factors that cause teacher/student confrontations in a pluralistic classroom.* Paper presented at the annual conference of the National Association of Minority Education, Seattle, WA. (ERIC Document Reproduction Service No. ED371089)

Sheets, R. H., & Gay, G. (1996, May). Student perceptions of disciplinary conflict in ethnically diverse classrooms. *NASSP Bulletin,* pp. 84–93.

Short, P. M., Short, R. J., & Blanton, C. (1994). *Rethinking school discipline: Alternatives that work.* Thousand Oaks, CA: Corwin Press.

Shure, M. B. (1992a). *I can problem solve: An interpersonal cognitive problem-solving program (intermediate elementary grades).* Champaign, IL: Research Press.

Shure, M. B. (1992b). *I can problem solve: An interpersonal cognitive problem-solving program (kindergarten & primary grades).* Champaign, IL: Research Press.

Shure, M. B. (1992c). *I can problem solve: An interpersonal cognitive problem-solving program (preschool).* Champaign, IL: Research Press.

Skiba, R. J., Peterson, R. L., & Williams, T. (1997). Office referrals and suspension: Disciplinary interventions in middle schools. *Education and Treatment of Children, 20*(3), 295–315.

Slavin, R. E. (1995). *Cooperative learning: Theory, research, and practice* (2nd ed.). Boston: Allyn & Bacon.

Slicker, E. K. (1998). Relationship of parenting style to behavioral adjustment in graduating high school seniors. *Journal of Youth and Adolescence, 27*(13), 345–372.

Smith, D. J., Young, R., West, R. P., Morgan, D. P., & Rhode, G. (1988). Reducing the disruptive behavior of junior high school students: A classroom self-management procedure. *Behavioral Disorders, 13,* 231–239.

Soar, R. S., & Soar, R. M. (1979). Emotional climate and management. In P. L. Peterson & H. J. Walberg (Eds.), *Research on teaching: Concepts, findings, and implications* (pp. 97–119). Berkeley, CA: McCutchan.

Stage, S. A., & Quiroz, D. R. (1997). A meta-analysis of interventions to decrease disruptive classroom behavior in public education settings. *School Psychology Review, 26*(3), 333–368.

Stanard, R. P. (2000). Assessment and treatment of adolescent depression and suicidality. *Journal of Mental Health Counseling, 22*(3), 204–217.

Stevens, K. B., Blackhurst, A. E., & Slaton, D. B. (1991). Teaching memorized spelling with a microcomputer: Time delay and computer-assisted instruction. *Journal of Applied Behavior Analysis, 24,* 153–160.

Sugai, G., & Colvin, G. (1996). Debriefing: A proactive addition to negative consequences for problem behavior. *Education and Treatment of Children, 20,* 209–221.

Thompson, R. A., & Wyatt, J. M. (1999). Current research on child maltreatment: Implications for educators. *Educational Psychology Review, 11*(3), 173–201.

Tobin, T. J., & Sugai, G. M. (1999). Using sixth-grade school records to predict school violence, chronic discipline problems, and high school outcomes. *Journal of Emotional and Behavioral Disorders, 7*(1), 40–53.

Trapani, C., & Gettinger, M. (1989). Effects of social skills training and cross-age tutoring on academic achievement and social behaviors of boys with learning disabilities. *Journal of Research and Development in Education, 22*(4), 1–9.

Vandell, D. L., & Hembree, S. E. (1994). Peer social status and friendship: Independent contributors to children's social and academic adjustment. *Merrill-Palmer Quarterly, 40*(4), 461–471.

Wang, M. C., Haertel, G. D., & Walberg, H. J. (1993). Toward a knowledge base for school learning. *Review of Educational Research, 63*(3), 249–294.

Ward, C. M. (1998). Student discipline and alleviating criminal behavior in the inner city. *The Urban Review, 30*(1), 29–49.

Weiner, J., Harris, P. J., & Shirer, C. (1990). Achievement and social-behavioral correlates of peer status in LD children. *Learning Disability Quarterly, 13*(2), 114–127.

Winborn, J. D. (1992, November). *A study of the effectiveness of a Saturday school in reducing suspension, expulsion, and corporal punishment.* Paper presented at the annual meeting of the Mid-south Educational Research Association, Knoxville, TN. (ERIC Document Reproduction Service No. ED355663)

Wlodkowski, R. J. (1982). *Discipline: The great false hope.* Milwaukee, WI: University of Wisconsin–Milwaukee. (ERIC Document Reproduction Service No. 224782)

Wolfgang, C. H. (1995). *Solving discipline problems: Methods and models for today's teachers* (3rd ed.). Boston: Allyn & Bacon.

Wolfgang, C. H., & Glickman, C. D. (1986). Solving discipline problems: Strategies for classroom teachers (2nd ed.). New York: Allyn & Bacon.

Wooster, A. (1986). Social skills training and reading gain. *Educational Research, 28*(1), 68–71.

Wright, S. P., Horn, S. P., & Sanders, W. L. (1997). Teacher and classroom context effects on student achievement: Implications for teacher evaluation. *Journal of Personnel Evaluation in Education, 11*, 57–67.

Wubbels, T., Brekelmans, M., van Tartwijk, J., & Admiral, W. (1999). Interpersonal relationships between teachers and students in the classroom. In H. C. Waxman & H. J. Walberg (Eds.), *New directions for teaching practice and research* (pp. 151–170). Berkeley, CA: McCutchan.

Wubbels, T., & Levy, J. (1993). *Do you know what you look like? Interpersonal relationships in education.* London: Falmer Press.

Zabel, M. K. (1986, November). Timeout use with behaviorally disordered students. *Behavioral Disorders,* 15–21.

Zoccolillo, M. (1993). Gender and development of conduct disorder. *Development and Psychopathology, 5*(1–2), 65–78.

INDEX

138

About the Authors

Robert J. Marzano is a Senior Scholar at Mid-Continent Research for Education and Learning in Aurora, Colorado; an Associate Professor at Cardinal Stritch University in Milwaukee, Wisconsin; Vice President of Pathfinder Education, Inc.; and President of Marzano & Associates consulting firm in Centennial, Colorado. He has developed programs and practices used in K–12 classrooms that translate current research and theory in cognition into instructional methods. An internationally known trainer and speaker, Marzano has authored 20 books and more than 150 articles and chapters on topics such as reading and writing instruction, thinking skills, school effectiveness, restructuring, assessment, cognition, and standards implementation. Recent ASCD titles include *What Works in Schools: Translating Research into Action* (2003); *A Handbook for Classroom Instruction That Works* (Marzano, Paynter, Pickering, & Gaddy, 2001); and *Classroom Instruction That Works: Research-Based Strategies for Increasing Student Achievement* (Marzano, Pickering, & Pollack, 2001). Additionally, Marzano headed a team of authors who developed *Dimensions of Learning* (ASCD, 1992). His most recent work is *The Pathfinder Project: Exploring the Power of One* (Pathfinder Education, Inc., 2003). Marzano received his B.A. in English from Iona College in New York, a M.Ed. in Reading/Language Arts from Seattle University, and a Ph.D. in Curriculum and Instruction from the University of Washington. He can be contacted at 7127 South Danube Court, Centennial, CO 80016. Phone: (303) 796-7683. E-mail: robertjmarzano@aol.com

Jana S. Marzano has been a psychotherapist in private practice in Colorado for more than 20 years. She is a Licensed Professional Counselor (LPC) and has a M.A. in Professional Psychology from the University of Northern Colorado in Greeley, Colorado, and a B.S. in Mental Health Services from Metropolitan State University in Denver. She has coauthored a book on vocabulary instruction published by the International Reading Association and has published a number of articles on topics ranging from classroom management to the role of the self-system in determining human behavior. Her areas of speciality include post-traumatic stress disorders, mood disorders, marital counseling, and substance and behavioral addictions. She works extensively with children and adolescents on a variety of issues. She can be contacted at 7127 South Danube Court, Centennial, CO 80016. Phone: (303) 220-1151. E-mail: janamarzano@aol.com.

Debra J. Pickering is a private consultant and Director of Staff Development in Littleton Public Schools, Littleton, Colorado. During more than 25 years in education, she has gained practical experience as a classroom teacher and district staff development coordinator and has done extensive consulting with administrators and teachers, K–12. Her work in research and development centers on the study of learning and the development of curriculum, instruction, and assessment that addresses clearly identified learning goals. With a combination of theoretical grounding and practical experience, she works with educators throughout the world who are attempting to translate theory into practice. Pickering has coauthored several articles and programs, including *Dimensions of Learning Teacher's Manual* (2nd ed.) and other materials for ASCD's *Dimensions of Learning* series, a comprehensive model of learning that provides a framework for developing students into independent learners and complex thinkers. She most recently coauthored *Classroom Instruction That Works: Research-Based Strategies for Increasing Student Achievement,* which summarizes decades of research on instruction and recommends specific instructional strategies for K–12 classrooms. She received a B.S. degree in English/Drama Education from the University of Missouri, an M.A. in School Administration from the University of Denver, and a Ph.D. in Curriculum and Instruction with an emphasis on Cognitive Psychology from the University of Denver. Pickering can be contacted at 10098 East Powers Ave., Englewood, CO 80111. Phone: (303) 694-9899. E-mail: djplearn@hotmail.com.

Related ASCD Resources: Classroom Management That Works: Research-Based Strategies for Every Teacher

At the time of publication, the following ASCD resources were available; for the most up-to-date information about ASCD resources, go to www.ascd.org. ASCD stock numbers are noted in parentheses.

Audiotapes

Applying Brain Stress Research to Classroom Management (4 Live Seminars on Tape) by Robert Sylwester (#297188)

Classroom Management at the Middle Grade Level by Alfred A. Arth, Judith Brough, Larry Holt, Kathleen B. Wheeler (#202239)

Conscious Classroom Management: Bringing Out the Best in Students and Teachers by Rick Smith (#202248)

Insights on Better Classroom Management from Brain Research by Eric Jensen (#299194)

Proactively Addressing Behavior and Discipline in an Urban Middle School: Implications and and Findings by Shelley Beech, Hank Edmonson, Nancy Hale, and Donna Wickham (#201183)

A Timely Approach to Using Proven Strategies for Dealing with Difficult Classroom Behaviors by Louise Griffith and Patricia Voss (#200075)

Using Data to Shape Classroom Practice by Richard DuFour (#299311)

Multimedia

Classroom Management/Positive School Climate Topic Pack (#198219)

Classroom Management Professional Inquiry Kit by Robert Hanson (eight activity folders and a videotape). (#998059)

Dimensions of Learning Complete Program (teacher's and trainer's manuals, book, 6 videos, and an additional free video) Educational consultants: Robert J. Marzano and Debra J. Pickering (#614239)

Networks

Visit the ASCD Web site (www.ascd.org) and search for "networks" for information about professional educators who have formed groups around topics like "Dimensions of Learning" and "Instructional Supervision." Look in the "Network Directory" for current facilitators' addresses and phone numbers.

Online Resources

Visit the ASCD Web site (www.ascd.org) for the following professional development opportunities:

Online Tutorial: *Classroom Management* (free)

Professional Development Online: *Classroom Management: Building Relationships for Better Learning, Dimensions of Learning,* and *What Works in Schools,* among others (for a small fee; password protected)

Print Products

Beyond Discipline: From Compliance to Community by Alfie Kohn (#196075)

Classroom Instruction That Works: Research-Based Strategies for Increasing Student Achievement by Robert J. Marzano, Debra J. Pickering, and Jane E. Pollock (#101010)

Discipline with Dignity by Richard L. Curwin and Allen N. Mendler (#199235)

Educating Oppositional and Defiant Children by Philip S. Hall and Nancy D. Hall (#103053)

Winning Strategies for Classroom Management by Carol Cummings (#100052)

A Handbook for Classroom Instruction That Works by Robert J. Marzano, Jennifer S. Norford, Diane E. Paynter, Debra J. Pickering, and Barbara B. Gaddy (#101041)

Key Elements of Classroom Management: Managing Time and Space, Student Behavior, and Instructional Strategies by Joyce McLeod, Jan Fisher, and Ginny Hoover (#103008) **(NEW!)**

The Results Fieldbook: Practical Strategies from Dramatically Improved Schools by Mike Schmoker (#101001)

What Works in Schools: Translating Research into Action by Robert J. Marzano (#102271)

Videos

How to Design Classroom Management to Enhance Learning (Tape 16 of How To Series) (#403114)

Managing Today's Classroom (3 videos with facilitator's guide) Educational consultant: Rheta DeVries (#498027)

What Works in Schools Video Series (3 videos) Educational consultant: Robert J. Marzano (#403047)

For more information, visit us on the World Wide Web (http://www.ascd.org), send an e-mail message to member@ascd.org, call the ASCD Service Center (1-800-933-ASCD or 703-578-9600, then press 2), send a fax to 703-575-5400, or write to Information Services, ASCD, 1703 N. Beauregard St., Alexandria, VA 22311-1714 USA.